Creating Web Pages
Weekend Crash Course™

Creating Web Pages
Weekend Crash Course™

Charlie Morris

Hungry Minds™

Best-Selling Books • Digital Downloads • e-Books • Answer Networks
e-Newsletters • Branded Web Sites • e-Learning

New York, NY • Cleveland, OH • Indianapolis, IN

Creating Web Pages Weekend Crash Course™
Published by
Hungry Minds, Inc.
909 Third Avenue
New York, NY 10022
www.hungryminds.com

Library of Congress Control Number: 2001092735
ISBN: 0-7645-4871-9
Printed in the United States of America
10 9 8 7 6 5 4 3 2 1
1B/RQ/QZ/QR/IN
Distributed in the United States by
Hungry Minds, Inc.
Distributed by CDG Books Canada Inc. for Canada; by Transworld Publishers Limited in the United Kingdom; by IDG Norge Books for Norway; by IDG Sweden Books for Sweden; by IDG Books Australia Publishing Corporation Pty. Ltd. for Australia and New Zealand; by TransQuest Publishers Pte Ltd. for Singapore, Malaysia, Thailand, Indonesia, and Hong Kong; by Gotop Information Inc. for Taiwan; by ICG Muse, Inc. for Japan; by Intersoft for South Africa; by Eyrolles for France; by International Thomson Publishing for Germany, Austria, and Switzerland; by Distribuidora Cuspide for Argentina; by LR International for Brazil; by Galileo Libros for Chile; by Ediciones ZETA S.C.R. Ltda. for Peru; by WS Computer Publishing Corporation, Inc., for the Philippines; by Contemporanea de Ediciones for Venezuela; by Express Computer Distributors for the Caribbean and West Indies; by Micronesia Media Distributor, Inc. for Micronesia; by Chips Computadoras S.A. de C.V. for Mexico; by Editorial Norma de Panama S.A. for Panama; by American Bookshops for Finland.

For general information on Hungry Minds' products and services please contact our Customer Care department within the U.S. at 800-762-2974, outside the U.S. at 317-572-3993 or fax 317-572-4002.

For sales inquiries and reseller information, including discounts, premium and bulk quantity sales, and foreign-language translations, please contact our Customer Care department at 800-434-3422, fax 317-572-4002 or write to Hungry Minds, Inc., Attn: Customer Care Department, 10475 Crosspoint Boulevard, Indianapolis, IN 46256.

For information on licensing foreign or domestic rights, please contact our Sub-Rights Customer Care department at 212-884-5000.

For information on using Hungry Minds' products and services in the classroom or for ordering examination copies, please contact our Educational Sales department at 800-434-2086 or fax 317-572-4005.

For press review copies, author interviews, or other publicity information, please contact our Public Relations department at 317-572-3168 or fax 317-572-4168.

For authorization to photocopy items for corporate, personal, or educational use, please contact Copyright Clearance Center, 222 Rosewood Drive, Danvers, MA 01923, or fax 978-750-4470.

About the Author

In 1994, **Charlie Morris** was working for a print magazine that was looking for a less expensive way to publish. Someone suggested trying a new medium called the World Wide Web, and *The Web Developer's Journal* became one of the first online magazines. Charlie had a major hand in turning *The Web Developer's Journal* into a respected authority on current Web development tools and techniques. Also, Charlie has created Web sites for many businesses both large and small and has written articles on Web design and multimedia for various print and online magazines. He lives in Florida with his wife and a Wussel cat.

Credits

Acquisitions Editor
Carol Sheehan

Project Editor
Chandani Thapa

Technical Editor
Chris Stone

Copy Editor
C. M. Jones

Editorial Manager
Colleen Totz

Project Coordinator
Dale White

Graphics and Production Specialists
Joyce Haughey, Adam Mancilla,
Betty Schulte, Brian Torwelle

Quality Control Technicians
Andy Hollandbeck, Carl Pierce,
Marianne Santy

Permissions Editor
Carmen Krikorian

Media Development Coordinator
Marisa Pearman

Proofreading and Indexing
TECHBOOKS Production Services

For Bruce and Kief, my longtime
partners in Web publishing

Preface

Creating *Web Pages Weekend Crash Course* teaches the reader to create a simple but functional Web site. One of the most appealing things about the Web is that it makes publishing content relatively easy. Unlike working with more traditional media such as print, audio, and video, creating Web sites requires no expensive equipment and little in the way of specialized expertise. Although Web sites can be incredibly complex, and many of today's high-profile sites have been created at enormous cost both in money and human ingenuity, the basic skills of Web publishing are simple enough that a person with basic computer skills can quickly learn enough to create a perfectly functional and useful Web site for home or business.

Indeed, these skills are demanded of more and more people as the Web evolves into one of the standard means of communication. Creating Web pages is no longer the exclusive province of computer experts (if it ever really was). Today's businessperson, regardless of the field or type of organization he or she works in, is expected to be a skilled user of the post office, telephone, fax, and e-mail. Increasingly, not only in business but even in personal life, you need to add Web skills to this list, and you need to acquire a knowledge not only of how to surf the Web but also of how to create your own content for Web distribution.

I have been involved with the Web since shortly after its public unveiling in 1994. In the early days of the Web, there was a pervasive, underground, do-it-yourself mentality. All or most of the tools used were free, and the most compelling Web sites were being created by young, self-taught designers in their spare bedrooms. Almost eight years later, the Web has become part of the mainstream, with huge corporations building hundred-million-dollar Web sites that receive millions of visitors each day. I would like to stress, however, that the *old Web* hasn't gone away. The adventurous spirit and the mentality of sharing and giving that have so captured the popular imagination are as strong as ever. Almost everything described in this book can be done with free software tools you can download from the Web. An incredibly vast amount of information for further study is available from thousands of Web sites, newsgroups, and mailing lists — all absolutely free.

The many benefits of the Web can be summed up in a single word: freedom. As you learn about the techniques and technologies that make the Web work, and as you begin to design your own Web sites, it's a good idea to keep in mind the various ways in which the Web is free of constraints and limitations that characterize other media.

- *Platform independence*. The Web is designed to be equally accessible to any type of computer or operating system. Your Web pages may be viewed not only by users of Windows, Macintosh, Unix, or Linux, but by people who aren't using a computer at all. The proliferation of different types of client devices is one of the strongest trends in computing today, and more and more Web content is being delivered to personal digital assistants (PDAs), mobile phones, televisions, and other noncomputer devices.

- *Open standards*. The basic technologies on which the Web is built (TCP/IP, HTTP, HTML) are not owned by any particular company but are freely available for all to use. Many key software products, such as Netscape's browser and Sun's Java programming language, are *open source*, which means that the source code is available to anyone who wishes to tinker with it and try to make improvements. This not only keeps costs low but also ensures that standards and tools are constantly improving, as interested developers from all over the world can offer their input.

- *Low costs*. Many design tools are free, and Web-site hosting services are affordable (at least in the United States). Anyone can be a Web publisher.

- *No geographic limitations*. To a Web browser, it makes not the slightest difference whether a Web site originates next door or on the other side of the world. In my career as a writer and editor, I've received reader comments from dozens of countries on every continent. Even the humblest Web site can reach a worldwide audience. To take advantage of this great opportunity, make your Web sites as universal as you can, avoiding unnecessary geographic constraints.

- *Minimal regulation*. There are authorities who regulate various technical aspects of the Web; for example, the InterNIC regulates domain names, and the World Wide Web Consortium (W3C) sets standards for HTML. However, no regulatory body has jurisdiction over all the technical aspects of the Web, still less over its content. Furthermore, the international nature of the Web means that national and local laws and regulations are often impossible to enforce.

With all this freedom, naturally, comes responsibility. Before we roll up our sleeves and start building a Web site, please take a moment to think about what it means to be a responsible member of the Web community. Obviously, this means refraining from using the Web for any illegal or unethical purpose and conforming to general standards of *netiquette* (Internet etiquette) in your dealings with other Web users. Also, I urge you to accept the responsibility of holding your Web-design work to a high level of quality.

As the old computing saw has it, "garbage in, garbage out." Anyone who has surfed the Web a lot knows that an awful lot of garbage is out there. Perhaps the ease and low cost of Web publishing makes it inevitable that a lot of low-quality material is on the Web: incorrect information; bad design; errors in spelling, grammar, and style; horrible-quality graphics and audio — all are shockingly common. Even large and respected organizations that would never accept so much as a comma out of place in a printed document regularly publish material on the Web that can be described only as amateurish.

So please don't be in too much of a hurry. Tell your story and use your creativity, but also take the time to ensure that your work is of high quality. Avoid improper HTML; check your Web sites thoroughly to ensure that they function as intended; don't compromise the quality of your graphics and other media, and proofread text carefully to eliminate typos, spelling errors, and bad grammar. If you follow the procedures described in this book, I am confident you will have no difficulty achieving these goals, and I shall feel proud to have had a hand in training a new generation of conscientious, skillful Web designers.

Whom Is This Book For?

This book is intended for anyone who wishes to learn the basics of Web-site design quickly. Whether you seek only a working knowledge, or whether you plan to use this book as a basis for more advanced studies, *Creating Web Pages Weekend Crash Course* gives you a solid grasp of the basics. This book does not go into great detail about any one aspect of the Web-site-creation process, but neither does it present any watered-down information or misleading shortcuts you will need to unlearn.

The reader is assumed to be fairly computer literate. You should be comfortable using the Windows or Macintosh operating system (as well as some basic applications such as word processors), and you should be familiar with basic Internet activities such as browsing the Web and using e-mail.

Because this is a book about Web-site design, not about the larger topic of Internet strategy, I assume you've already made the decision to create a Web site, and I leave the question of what sort of content to include on your Web site up to you. Topics such as the business case for a Web site, the marketing of Web sites, and revenue models for Web sites are not within the scope of this book.

Also, this book does not contain a comprehensive HTML reference. The HTML code examples are intended to teach you important design concepts quickly, but there is not enough room to mention all of the hundreds of existing HTML elements. A thorough HTML reference, which lists all tags and their possible attributes, makes a valuable companion. Reference material of this kind is available not only in book form but at various free Web sites and is included in the help section of some full-featured HTML editing software. Addresses of several online HTML references are in Appendix C on the companion CD-ROM.

How to Use This Book

This book is divided into 30 sessions, each of which should take in the general area of a half hour to complete. Of course, you may proceed at your own pace, and you may find that some sessions take more or less time than predicted. Take as much time as you need to ensure that you understand the material presented in each session before proceeding to the next.

Each session builds on previous ones and refers to an example Web site, which starts off as a very simple site and grows gradually into a fairly complex site. Specific techniques and general design concepts are introduced little by little along the way. For maximum benefit, the sessions should be read in order.

Readers who already have some basic Web-design knowledge may feel safe skimming through the first few sessions, but I recommend giving them at least a cursory look for two reasons. First, even experts can learn something new about the basics that they missed the first time around. Second, I introduce certain concepts and terminology in the early sessions that are applied again and again in later sessions.

Overview

Creating Web Pages Weekend Crash Course consists of 30 timed chapters (sessions) divided into six parts, as follows.

Friday evening

This part contains four sessions that explain the basic concept of a Web site and introduce HyperText Markup Language (HTML) and the tools you need to work with it. You create a simple Web page and learn some design considerations to keep in mind.

Saturday morning

These six sessions introduce several additional text-formatting techniques. You learn to create Web graphics and incorporate them into a Web page.

Saturday afternoon

In these six sessions, you learn to arrange text on a page through the use of columns and white space. You also learn to divide a Web page into frames and to provide mechanisms for user feedback.

Saturday evening

This section consists of four sessions that explain how to use Cascading Style Sheets (CSS), as well as how to design a site that is well laid out and easy to use.

Sunday morning

These six sessions introduce you to advanced Web multimedia, including animations, image maps, audio, video, and scripting.

Sunday afternoon

These final four sessions discuss how to maintain a Web site and introduce the concept of dynamic-page generation. Finally, I discuss some overriding principles of quality Web design and provide suggestions for further study.

Appendixes

There are four appendixes: Appendixes A and B are in the book, and Appendixes C and D are on the CD-ROM. These appendixes provide the answers to review questions, a list of the material contained on the included CD-ROM, a list of links to useful Web resources for reference and further study, and a discussion of user compatibility issues.

Layout and Features

Symbols such as the one to the left appear in the margin to let you know how far along you are in each session. They are provided only as a tool to help you measure your progress, so don't worry if you fall behind or rush ahead from time to time.

30 Min. To Go

The ⇨ symbol is used to indicate a menu choice, such as: File ⇨ Save. Monospaced font is used to indicate programming code within the body text, such as `<TITLE>Freddy's Fishing Guide</TITLE>`.

Special notes, tips, and other bits of information are included at strategic points throughout the book and are indicated by individual icons.

Notes provide information that amplifies and expands upon information presented in the main text. They may refer you to further information about a certain topic, explain an apparent contradiction, or discuss situations only some readers face, such as an issue that applies only to a certain operating system.

Tips indicate a handy technique that, although not required, may help you save time or accomplish needed tasks more easily.

When you see "Never," I am warning you to avoid a certain way of doing things that could cause problems later on.

A Cross-Reference indicates a pointer to material discussed in another session.

CD-ROM indicates that a software product or an example of a technique discussed in the text is contained on the included CD-ROM.

Acknowledgments

Creating a book such as this requires a lot of hard work and attention to detail from a number of people.

Thanks to everyone at Hungry Minds, especially Carol Sheehan, Acquisitions Editor, and Chandani Thapa, Project Editor.

I'd also like to thank all the vendors whose products I discuss (and use), especially Macromedia, Jasc, and Adobe, for all their help and for making such fine products. Special thanks to Internet.com for assembling such a huge collection of free resources for Web developers.

And last, thanks to my wife, Denise, for providing support services and for her infinite patience during the birth of this book.

Contents at a Glance

Contents

Creating Web Pages
Weekend Crash Course™

☑ **Friday**

☐ Saturday

☐ Sunday

PART

I

Friday Evening

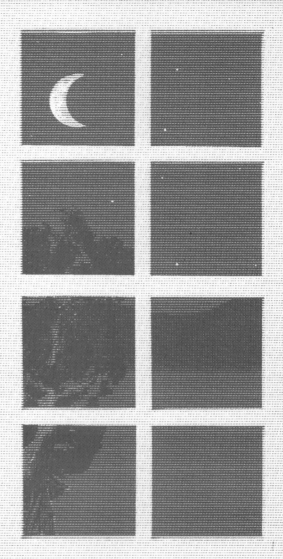

Creating Web Pages Using HTML

Session Checklist

✔	Introducing HTML
✔	Understanding HTML tags
✔	Understanding types of Web editors

**30 Min.
To Go**

The most important tool in a Web designer's toolbox is HyperText Markup Language (HTML). Often erroneously called a programming language, HTML is a markup language that tells a Web browser how to display the various elements of a Web page. You'll be happy to know that a markup language such as HTML is far easier to learn than a programming language such as BASIC, C++, or Java. In fact, you can learn to build a simple Web page by using HTML in a few easy steps.

Building Your First Web Page

To create Web pages by using HTML, you need two software tools:

1. *A word processor or text editor.* HTML files are simple text files, and they can be edited using any application that can save text files. Windows users can use Notepad, a simple word-processing application included in the Windows operating system. The equivalent for Mac users is called Simple Text (replaced in the new Mac OS X by an application called Text Edit).

2. *A Web browser.* A Web browser is the application used to view Web pages. The two most popular Web browsers, Netscape and Microsoft Internet Explorer, are free and come in several versions for various operating systems. You can download a browser from one of the following sites:

   a. Netscape 6: `http://home.netscape.com/download/`

   b. Internet Explorer 5.5: `http://www.microsoft.com/windows/ie/default.htm`

   c. Internet Explorer for Mac: `http://www.microsoft.com/mac/products/ie/`

   d. Opera 5: `http://www.opera.com/`

You can find even more browsers at `http://dir.yahoo.com/Computers_and_Internet/Software/Internet/World_Wide_Web/Browsers/`.

Follow these steps to create a simple Web page:

1. Launch your word processor. (Windows users choose Start ➪ Programs ➪ Accessories ➪ Notepad.)

2. Type the following text, exactly as shown in Listing 1-1:

Listing 1-1:

```
Hello, universe!
<BR>
<B>Hello, bold universe!</B>
```

Every example in this book that has a listing number is on the accompanying CD-ROM in the directory html_examples.

Figure 1-1 shows this file in Notepad.

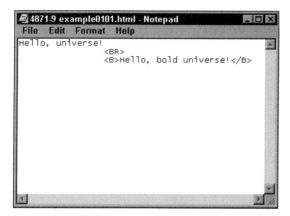

Figure 1-1
Using Notepad to edit an HTML file

3. Create a new directory on your hard drive for your example Web pages, and save this file to the new directory. Save it as a plain text file, but give it an .html file extension. For example, you might call it temp.html. Some word processors may give you the option of saving as an HTML file or as a Web page. *Do not* select this option. To be editable, the file must be saved as plain text. Figure 1-2 shows the Save dialog box.

HTML files can have a file extension of either .html or .htm. For example, temp.html and temp.htm are both valid names for an HTML file. There's little reason to prefer one over the other, but I recommend sticking to one or the other within a given Web site.

Figure 1-2
Saving the file in Notepad. Note that the file type is plain text, but the file extension is .html.

4. Launch your Web browser (Netscape, Microsoft Internet Explorer, Opera or one of the other available products).

5. Open the file you have saved. Internet Explorer users choose File ⇨ Open ⇨ Browse. Netscape users, choose File ⇨ Open File. Navigate through your directory structure until you find the file temp.html; open it by double-clicking the file name.

6. Figure 1-3 shows how the file appears in a Web browser. Different systems display Web pages differently; the page may not appear exactly as it does in Figure 1-3, but you should see two lines of text: the first line plain, the second line bold.

Figure 1-3
Viewing the example HTML file in Microsoft Internet Explorer

20 Min. To Go

Introducing Tags

Congratulations! You've created your first Web page. It's nothing fancy, but it will do as an example of how the HTML source code (what you see in your word processor) translates into the page you can view in your Web browser. To learn how this works, take another look at Listing 1-1:

```
Hello, universe!
<BR>
<B>Hello, bold universe!</B>
```

HTML uses *tags* to describe how text is to be displayed on a Web page. This example includes two tags: the Break (BR) tag, which creates a line break after the first line, and the Bold (B) tag, which makes the second line appear in bold type.

All HTML tags have certain characteristics:

- A tag always begins with a left-angle bracket (<) and ends with a right-angle bracket (>).

- Tags are not case-sensitive. <B> and <b> are interchangeable. However, it is common to use all caps for tags to make them stand out from the text; I follow this convention throughout this book.

Many tags, including the B tag of this example, are designed to be used in pairs: an opening and a closing tag. A closing tag has a slash immediately following the left angle bracket, thus:

Opening Bold tag: `<B>`

Closing Bold tag: `</B>`

All content between the opening and closing tags is affected by these tags, making the text appear bold in this example.

Editing and Viewing HTML Files

Compare Figure 1-1 with Figure 1-3. The same file is displayed in both, but the word processor displays the HTML code while the Web browser displays the Web page the code describes. This illustrates an important concept. An HTML file can be opened in two ways: it can be *viewed* or *edited*. When you view an HTML file in a Web browser, the content is presented according to the rules the tags specify. The tags themselves are invisible.

If, on the other hand, you open an HTML file by using a text-editing application, you see the raw HTML source code, including the tags. A markup language such as HTML enables you to separate *content* from *presentation*. To better understand this important concept, imagine a human editor using a pen to mark sections of text to indicate to the printer how the text should be printed. The editor sends this note to the printer:

Please print the following in bold type: "Hello universe!"

In this example, the content is between the quotation marks, and the preceding phrase instructs the printer as to the presentation of this content. In HTML, instead of using a pen, you use tags. The same instruction is expressed thus:

```
<B>Hello universe!</B>
```

The B tag is like a note to the Web browser that the content between the tags should be presented in bold type.

You can see the HTML source code behind any Web page simply by selecting the View Source feature in your Web browser. This can be a valuable learning tool, as you can see how any page on the Web has been built and get ideas to use in designing your own pages.

1. Connect to the Internet.
2. Launch your Web browser, and navigate to your favorite Web site.

3. In Internet Explorer, select View ⇨ Source. In Netscape, select View ⇨ Page Source or CTRL+U.

4. A new window opens that contains the HTML source code of the Web page.

**10 Min.
To Go**

Types of Web-Page Editors

So far, you've used a simple word processor to edit HTML files. But three types of applications can be used to create and edit HTML documents. Each has its own advantages and disadvantages, and Web designers often have strong opinions as to which is best.

Text editors

HTML files are nothing more than text files. In fact, you can convert a plain text file to an HTML file, and vice versa, simply by changing the file extension. Any word processor, or any other application that allows you to edit and save text files, can be used to create Web pages.

HTML editors

Editing HTML in a word processor is a tedious process, as you must either type tags manually or cut and paste them as desired. Tags can get very long and complex, and this can mean a lot of repetitive and tedious work that computers are supposed to free us from. Many HTML editors are available that offer various shortcuts to make editing faster.

An HTML editor is just a word processor that has shortcuts built in for the most common tags. The best HTML editors let you build tags by selecting options from dialog boxes, thus freeing you not only from typing but from remembering how to spell each tag and attribute. In fact, a good HTML editor can help you write better HTML by warning you if you do something improper.

Many HTML editors are available. Allaire's Homesite (http://allaire.com/Products/HomeSite/) is one of the most popular commercial products, but many cheap or free editors are available that are quite adequate. Some of the options, with addresses where you can download them from the Web, are:

- 1st Page 2000, from Evrsoft: http://www.evrsoft.com/download/
- Agile HTML Editor, from Compware: http://www.agilic.com/editor.htm

- BBedit for Mac OS X, from Bare Bones Software: `http://www.barebones.com/`

Figure 1-4 shows an HTML file being edited with Homesite.

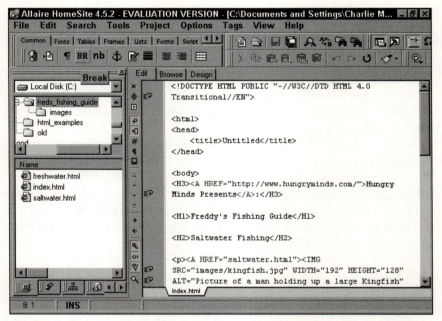

Figure 1-4
Using Homesite to edit an HTML file. Note the various icons across the top for inserting common tags and performing other often-repeated tasks.

WYSIWYG editors

Most people have become used to easy-to-use graphical operating systems such as Windows and the Macintosh OS and thus tend to see coding HTML as a throwback to an earlier, less user-friendly era of computing. Indeed, creating a Web document with HTML is obviously less intuitive and more tedious than creating a document with a modern word processor or desktop publishing (DTP) application. In response to the demand for higher-level Web-editing tools, several companies have developed so-called WYSIWYG (What You See Is What You Get) editors. A WYSIWYG editor (often incorrectly called an HTML editor) allows you to view a Web page and edit it at the same time by dragging and dropping elements on screen just as you do with a DTP package.

WYSIWYG editors are designed to be very easy to learn and use. They allow you to create pages without knowing the details of HTML or even having to edit the HTML code directly. Why would anyone wish to use a mere HTML editor, much less a lowly text editor? The fact is that WYSIWYG editors have some serious disadvantages. The code they generate tends to be unnecessarily complex, and often includes proprietary tags that aren't supported by all browsers. WYSIWYG editors have been controversial since they first began to appear, and many professional Web designers have nothing but scorn for them.

The important thing to remember is that a WYSIWYG editor is a sort of translator. Unlike a DTP program, which can store data in a proprietary format, the final output of any Web editor *must* be HTML. A WYSIWYG editor translates your on-screen editing actions into HTML — an inexact process that can result in improper code or in code that is difficult or impossible to edit manually later.

An even graver disadvantage for the student is that using a WYSIWYG editor shields you from learning HTML, the essential language on which the Web is based. This disadvantage is analogous to trying to learn to play the piano with the aid of a mechanical device that picks out the chords for you. Once you've mastered at least the basics of HTML, there's no reason not to try using a WYSIWYG editor if you like. But heed the voice of experience: if you use a WYSIWYG editor as a crutch, trying to avoid having to learn HTML, you could be sorry later. Figure 1-5 shows an HTML file being edited in Dreamweaver, a popular WYSIWYG editor.

Some of the best Web editors, such as Homesite and Dreamweaver, give you the best of both worlds, as each includes both an HTML editor and a WYSIWYG editor. All of the design techniques in this book can be accomplished with any of the various types of Web editors. For its educational value, I recommend starting with a simple text editor. Typing HTML code manually helps you retain the syntax and usage in your memory. Once you've mastered the basics, however, experiment with various editors, and use whichever suits your personal preference.

Evaluation versions of BBedit (an HTML editor for the Mac) and Dreamweaver (a WYSIWYG editor) can be found on the companion CD-ROM.

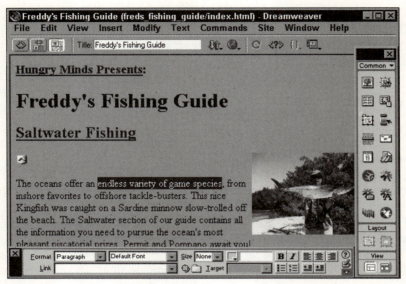

Figure 1-5
Editing a Web page with Dreamweaver. Note the various editing tools, similar to what you find in a DTP package.

Sophisticated word processors (such as Microsoft Word) can be used to edit HTML files either in text mode or in WYSIWYG mode. Be careful about opening HTML files to edit in Word. If you open an HTML file with Word, it acts as a not-very-good WYSIWYG editor. If you wish to use Word to edit an HTML file in the usual text-based fashion, you must open it as a .txt or .doc file.

Done!

REVIEW

In this session, you have encountered HTML and the concept of using it to create and edit Web pages. You should now understand:

- The purpose of HTML tags and their basic characteristics
- How to edit and preview an HTML file
- The various types of applications that can be used to edit HTML files

QUIZ YOURSELF

1. What language are Web pages built on? (See "Building Your First Web Page.")

2. What two software tools are needed to create a Web page? (See "Building Your First Web Page.")

3. What is the difference between viewing and editing an HTML file? (See "Editing and Viewing HTML Files.")

4. What are the three types of Web editors? (See "Types of Web-Page Editors.")

5. If you really want to impress HTML syntax and usage on your memory, which type of editor should you use? (See "Types of Web-Page Editors.")

Building a Simple Web Page

Session Checklist

✔ Learning basic tags common to every Web page

✔ Arranging text by using line breaks

✔ Organizing text by using heading tags

**30 Min.
To Go**

I n Session 1, you have learned the basic characteristics of HTML and have prac-
ticed using HTML tags to *mark up* text (that is, to indicate how text should be
presented in a Web browser). In this session, you expand on that knowledge
to create a complete page and add more text-formatting tags to your HTML
vocabulary.

Creating a Complete Web Page

Four tags must be included in every HTML document.

   1. The HTML tag defines a text file as an HTML document. The HTML tag
encloses the entire document (that is, the document begins with the
opening HTML tag and ends with the closing HTML tag).

2. The HEAD element (the section enclosed by the opening and closing HEAD tags) contains information about the document. Information contained in the HEAD section is not displayed on the Web page.

3. The TITLE tag, included within the HEAD section, provides an official title for the document. This title is not displayed on the Web page but may appear in the browser's title bar and in a user's list of Bookmarks or Favorites. In later sessions, you'll learn about other elements that may be included in the HEAD section.

4. The BODY element (the section enclosed by the opening and closing BODY tags) contains the content of the document.

As you have learned in Session 1, most browsers display a page correctly even if these elements are omitted. However, when using some of the advanced techniques that you'll learn in later sessions, a page may not be displayed as desired unless these elements are used correctly, so make a habit of using them in every page you design.

Type Listing 2-1 into your word processor or HTML editor, and you have created a complete Web page:

Listing 2-1:

```
<HTML>
    <HEAD>
        <TITLE>A Simple Web Page</TITLE>
    </HEAD>
    <BODY>
Hello, Universe!
    </BODY>
</HTML>
```

If you are using an HTML editor, this set of tags may be generated automatically as part of a new document template. If you are using a simple word processor, you may wish to save Listing 2-1 to use as a template for new pages.

Save this file to the subdirectory you have created in Session 1, giving it a file-name of index.html. To see what this file looks like as a Web page, launch your Web browser, and choose File ⇨ Open; then find and open the file. Figure 2-1 shows how the page appears in Netscape 6.0. Depending on your browser and local system settings, the page may not appear exactly the same on your computer, but you should see the words "Hello, Universe!" as plain, black text on a white background.

Figure 2-1
This is what the code in Listing 2-1 translates into when displayed in Netscape's browser. Notice that only the content between the BODY tags is displayed on screen and that the content between the TITLE tags is displayed in the title bar of the browser.

Not bad for 10 minutes of work but pretty basic. To make your text more attractive and easier to read, you need to use formatting tags. All formatting (controlling the appearance of text and where it appears on the page) must be done by using tags. This is an important point to understand: using more than one space, line breaks (carriage returns), and other formatting in HTML code does not affect the appearance of the resulting Web page.

For example, you can type "Hello Universe!" any way you like in your HTML code:

```
Hello Universe!

Hello          Universe!

Hello
Universe!
```

All three of these are displayed exactly the same way when the Web page is viewed in a browser. To view changes you make to an HTML file, you must save the file; then choose Refresh (or Reload) in your browser.

**20 Min.
To Go**

Marking Up Body Text by Using P and BR Tags

Fortunately, a wide variety of tags can control the way text and other elements appear on a Web page. One of the most basic is the BR (Break) tag, which creates a single line break. The following code causes each sentence to appear on its own line:

```
Hello Universe!
<BR>Do you love to fish?
```

Note that the BR tag is a standalone tag (that is, it has no corresponding closing tag). Also note that, as explained previously, the way you format the HTML code itself makes no difference in the appearance of the Web page. The following code yields the same result:

```
Hello Universe!<BR>Do you love to fish?
```

Multiple BR tags can be used to create multiple line breaks. For example:

```
Hello Universe!
<BR><BR><BR><BR>
Do you love to fish?
```

The P (Paragraph) tag creates a double line break, which is the standard way of indicating a new paragraph in an HTML document.

```
Hello Universe!

<P>Do you love to fish?

<P>We sure do!
```

The P tag has an optional closing tag. In the following example, the second line of text uses the closing P tag, but the third line of text omits it. Both should work equally well.

```
Hello Universe!

<P>Do you love to fish?</P>
```

```
<P>We sure do!
```

In printed media, it's customary to set off a paragraph by indenting the first line, not by using a double line break. In Web pages, however, it's far more common to set off a paragraph by using a double line break and no indent (which is what the P tag does by default). Most Web designers agree that this makes text easier to read on a Web page. In Session 5, you learn how to create indents by using the   character. You can also create indents by using Cascading Style Sheets (CSS), which you'll meet in Session 17.

You can create a double line break by using two BR tags, but this is not the correct way to set off a paragraph. Using the P tag is preferable for two reasons, one theoretical and the other practical:

1. HTML tags should refer to the type of element they modify, rather than specifying the exact formatting to be applied to that element. The P tag tells the browser that the following text is a paragraph but leaves the decision as to how a paragraph break should be formatted up to the browser. This distinction may not be clear at the moment, but you learn its importance in Session 17.

2. The BR tag always creates a single line break, regardless of which tags come before or after it. As you will see in the next section, a Heading tag forces a double line break. Therefore, if you use BR tags to set off paragraphs, you need to have a pair of BR tags at the beginning of every paragraph that *does not* follow a heading and no BR tags at the beginning of every paragraph that *does* follow a heading (otherwise, four line breaks appear after each heading). Confusing? Yes, and a lot of unnecessary work as well. The P tag is intelligent enough to insert line breaks only when they are not already forced by another tag. Use P to set off every paragraph, and the desired double line break always appears.

**10 Min.
To Go**

Using Headings to Organize Content: the H1 through H6 Tags

Every designer knows you can make text far easier to read by dividing it into organized sections, each with its own heading. In HTML, you can do this by using Heading (H1, H2, H3, H4, H5 and H6) tags. Type the following example into your HTML editor; then see how it looks in your browser.

```
<H1>Freddy's Fishing Guide</H1>

<H2>Saltwater Fishing</H2>

<P>The oceans offer an endless variety of game species, from
inshore tasties to offshore tackle-busters.

<H2>Freshwater Fishing</H2>

<P>Some of the most avidly pursued fish swim in fresh water, from
the majestic trout and salmon of northern waters to the wily
largemouth bass.
```

Note that all Heading tags *must* have both opening and closing tags. Also note that a Heading tag normally forces a double line break regardless of whether the Heading tag is followed by a P tag, but it is correct form to include the P tag as you do in the previous example.

 Although the formatting of your HTML code does not affect the formatting of the Web page, it's a good idea when writing any computer language to use line breaks and indents to make the code easier to read and to edit.

Good style dictates that you use Heading tags in strict hierarchical order (that is, H1 should be followed by H2, then by H3, and so on). However, in certain cases, you can create special effects by juxtaposing Heading tags. Listing 2-2 includes an intro line above the main heading. The result is shown in Figure 2-2.

Listing 2-2:

```
<HTML>

   <HEAD>
      <TITLE>Freddy's Fishing Guide</TITLE>
   </HEAD>

   <BODY>

<H3>Fish Incorporated Presents:</H3>
<H1>Freddy's Fishing Guide</H1>
```

```
<H2>Saltwater Fishing</H2>

<P>The oceans offer an endless variety of game species, from
inshore favorites to offshore tackle-busters.

    <H2>Freshwater Fishing</H2>

<P>Some of the most avidly pursued fish swim in fresh water, from
the majestic trout and salmon of northern waters to the wily
largemouth bass.

    </BODY>

</HTML>
```

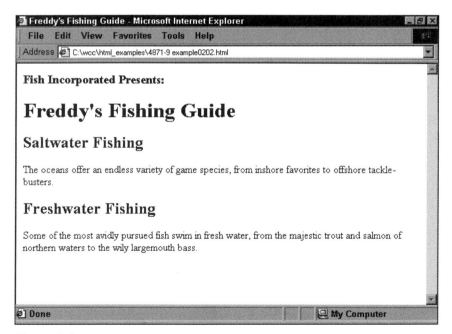

Figure 2-2
You've constructed a functional and easy-to-read Web page by using the
Paragraph and Heading tags only. Many existing sites consist of little more.

Done!

REVIEW

In this session, you have learned to create a simple-text Web page. This includes:

- Defining a Web page by using the HTML, HEAD, TITLE and BODY tags.
- Creating line breaks by using the P and BR tags.
- Organizing text by using Heading tags.

QUIZ YOURSELF

1. What is contained in the HEAD section of an HTML document?
    (See "Creating a Complete Web Page.")

2. What is contained in the BODY section of an HTML document?
    (See "Creating a Complete Web Page.")

3. How do you create a set of four line breaks in an HTML document? (See
    "Marking Up Body Text by Using P and BR Tags.")

4. What type of formatting is generally used to set off a new paragraph in
    an HTML document? What tag do you use to create this formatting? (See
    "Marking Up Body Text by Using P and BR Tags.")

5. What is the effect of following a Heading tag with a Paragraph tag? (See
    "Using Headings to Organize Content: the H1 through H6 Tags.")

Publishing on the Web

Session Checklist

✔	Understanding Web servers
✔	Establishing your presence on the Web
✔	Web addresses and URLs

**30 Min.
To Go**

You've learned to use HTML to create pages that can be viewed by using a Web browser; in addition, you've learned a few ways to organize text on a page. But it isn't really a worldwide Web site until it's available to the public over the Internet. In this session, you learn to establish a Web presence and to publish your files on the Web.

Web Servers and Hosting Accounts

The term *Web* refers to the subset of the Internet based on *HyperText Transfer Protocol* (HTTP), which allows the display of text, graphics, and other media. Other features of the Internet, such as e-mail, newsgroups, or *File Transfer Protocol*

(FTP), are not (strictly speaking) part of the Web, although often they have close relationships with Web sites.

Making information available worldwide

Web sites can be very complex, but the basic concept is simple: A Web site is a group of computer files stored on a powerful computer called a Web server. These files can be accessed by many users over a network.

Usually, a *Web server* is defined as a computer that is permanently connected to the Internet or to some other computer network and allows remote users to access files stored on its hard drives. *Server* refers both to the computer itself and to the software that allows it to make content available on the Web. Apache, Netscape Server, and Internet Information Server (IIS) are examples of Web-server software packages.

Files can be viewed by three different means:

1. *On a local machine*. You can open Web files on a local machine, as you have learned to do in Sessions 1 and 2. Typically, you view newly created or edited files on your local machine to test them before uploading the final versions to your Web server.

2. *Over the public Internet*. Once a file is placed on a Web server that has a permanent Internet connection, anyone who has Internet access can view it.

3. *Over a private network*. Some Web sites are created for use over a private Local Area Network (LAN) or Wide Area Network (WAN). Such an arrangement is often called an *intranet*. The process of creating and serving Web content is the same for both public and private networks. Almost all of the design techniques discussed in this book apply to intranets as well as to public Web sites.

Web-hosting services

You may be happy to learn that you need little or no network expertise to create and maintain a Web site. Of course, an understanding of how networks and Web servers work is very useful to a Web designer, but here we are concerned only with designing and building Web sites themselves; we must limit our discussion of networking and hosting to information you need to get a Web site up and running on a server.

Any network-capable computer can act as a Web server, and some hardy souls choose to set up their own. However, the complexity of maintaining Web servers in a reliable and secure manner leads most Web-site owners to hire an *Internet Service Provider* (ISP), also known as a *hosting service*. ISPs store your Web content on their servers, making your Web content available over the Internet.

Note that having Web *access* is not the same as having a Web *presence*. Web access, whether it consists of a dial-up connection or a faster connection such as cable or DSL, allows you to view existing Web content on your local computer. Web presence means that you own content available on a public Web server and that you are able to replace or update it as desired.

Often, you can purchase both types of services from the same ISP, and many people do, especially for personal Web sites. However, an Internet-access account and a hosting account are separate services and may be purchased from different providers. You will probably choose a local ISP for your Internet-access account to avoid paying long-distance charges. A hosting provider, however, can be located anywhere in the world. There's no real reason for you to prefer a host that is close to your geographic location or even to know where the ISP's servers are located. Figure 3-1 shows the connection between the user of a Web site and the files that make up the site, stored on a Web server.

There are many Web-hosting services, catering to all types of Web-site owners. The best place to shop for one is on the Web itself. Several sites publish listings of ISPs and enable you to search for one that meets your desired criteria in terms of features and pricing. ISPs offer different pricing plans based on bandwidth (how many users visit your site in a given time period) and storage (how much disk space you need to store the files that make up your site). The lowest-priced plan is usually more than adequate for a personal or small-business site, but a larger site or one with a lot of visitors needs more server capacity, and thus costs more.

Whatever plan you choose, make sure it includes unlimited FTP access to your site (as discussed later in this session). Never agree to a plan that makes you pay a fee for making changes to your site. And if an ISP doesn't give you good service, take your business elsewhere; there are plenty of good companies to choose from.

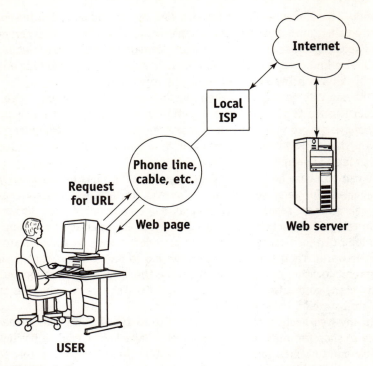

Figure 3-1
The user requests a particular Web page, and his or her local ISP relays this request via the Internet to the appropriate Web server, which responds by sending the page back to the user. Both request and response may pass through many computers and network paths on the way to their final destinations, but this process is transparent to the user.

 Try The List of ISPs (http://www.thelist.com), or go to an online directory such as Yahoo (http://www.yahoo.com) or The Open Directory (http://www.dmoz.org) and search for hosting services.

A good hosting service should be able to walk you through all the steps of establishing an account, and you should be able to start posting files on the Web within a couple of days at most. However, there's no need to wait to start designing Web pages. Everything in this book can be done on your local computer, and the files can be made live on the Internet by uploading them to a Web server at any time.

From here on, I'll assume you have established a hosting account or that your company is providing you with access to one. If you're working on an intranet site, your organization's internal servers are conceptually equivalent to the external ISP. Later in this session, you learn to send files to and from your Web server to create and edit your Web site.

Establishing a Web Presence

**20 Min.
To Go**

Establishing a Web presence is getting easier all the time. Plenty of reputable hosting services can walk you through the process painlessly. Establishing and maintaining a Web site is not expensive compared to the costs of publishing in most other media. The process consists of three steps:

1. Choose an ISP, and establish a Web-hosting account.
2. Register a domain name for your site if you so desire.
3. The ISP configures its servers so that your domain name points to the location of your Web files.

Once these steps have been completed, you are ready to transfer your HTML documents to the live Web server. Once you've done that, they'll be available to the public over the Internet. Note that, unlike most of the step-by-step procedures presented in this book, this one is not completed in half an hour. You need to spend some time shopping around before you choose an appropriate ISP; then you have to wait for the ISP to get your hosting account and domain name set up. Any of the better hosting services, however, should be able to handle all three steps for you in a matter of days, if not hours.

About Domain Names

Just as each postal customer has a unique street address, every Web server has a unique Internet Protocol (IP) address. An IP address consists of four numbers separated by periods; they are occasionally seen in URLs, as in this example:

```
http://198.41.0.196
```

Typing the preceding address into your browser's address bar takes you to Network Solutions' Web site.

To save us all from the drudgery of having to remember such numeric addresses, the system of domain names has been invented. A domain name is an alpha-numeric name that can be set up to point to a specific IP address and thus to a specific Web site. Because each domain name must be unique, the InterNIC, one of the bodies that oversees the Internet, maintains a record of the registered owner of each domain name. Network Solutions, whose site you visited in the preceding example, used to be the only company that handled registering domain names with the InterNIC. Today various companies act as registrars and can register a domain name with the InterNIC for you for a yearly fee.

Must you have your own domain name to have a Web site? Not at all. A Web site is simply a group of files, and there is no limit to the number of files that can be listed under a domain. Many of the large service providers, such as America Online (AOL) and GeoCities, host many member Web sites under their domain. The URL for a site hosted on AOL might look like this:

```
http://www.aol.com/~johndoe/index.html
```

The tilde (~) is a tip-off that this site is a "user account" at an ISP. Because of the ease of remembering a simpler URL and the additional prestige of having your own domain name, most businesses choose to register and use their own domain names. Once you've registered a domain name or arranged to use an existing one, your ISP must establish a link between the domain name and your Web content. They do this by configuring a specialized server called a Domain Name Server (DNS) so that your domain name points to the location in which your home page is stored on their servers.

A single domain name doesn't always correspond to a single Web site. Many companies, especially large ones, register multiple domain names but set them up so that they all point to the same home page.

Understanding URLs

So a file that resides on a Web server can be viewed by anyone who has an Internet connection and Web-browser software: *if* that person knows the correct address. Just as a letter requires a street address to reach its destination and a telephone number is required to reach someone on the telephone, an Internet user must use the proper address to view a particular Web page.

This address is called a *Uniform Resource Locater* (URL). A URL specifies the name and location of a file, which is requested from a Web server when the user types the URL into a browser's address field or clicks a hyperlink containing the URL. You can get an idea of how Web content is organized by examining the parts of a typical URL.

```
http://www.wackypages.com/adverts/seafu.html
```

1. `http://` This part tells the server to send a file by using the HTTP protocol. This section begins all Web URLs.

2. `www.wackypages.com` This is the domain name of the site. It identifies the server on which the requested file is located.

3. `/adverts/seafu.html` This is the path and file name of the requested file. Files on a Web server are organized into directories (folders) just as they are on a computer. Note, however, that Web addresses always use the forward slash (/), *not* the backslash (\) to indicate subdirectories.

By convention, the home page of a Web site is index.html. Usually, Web-server software is configured so that if a user requests the domain name by itself, without specifying a file name, the file index.html is displayed. Of course, you can direct visitors to any page you like by specifying a file name in the URL. Also, you can configure your Web-server software so that it recognizes any file specified as the home page.

As we all know, computers are very literal-minded. Even a tiny mistake such as a space (spaces aren't permitted in URLs) or a single slash where a double slash should be, will prevent the desired page from being loaded. If a page fails to appear, triple-check the URL before you assume there's something wrong with the Web server.

10 Min. To Go

Exchanging Files with Your Web Server

Once you've created a Web page, it must be stored on your Web server to make it available over the Web. The process of copying files to your server is referred to as *uploading*. This is done by using File Transfer Protocol (FTP), which requires a software application called an FTP client.

Windows 2000 comes with an FTP client, but it is a command-line tool and awkward for large file transfers. I prefer a graphical, drag-and-drop FTP client such as LeapFTP.

LeapFTP is included on the companion CD-ROM.

To make a connection to the server, you need the following information, which you must obtain from your ISP or network administrator:

- Server IP address or name (usually your domain name)
- User name
- Password

Good FTP clients let you save the preceding information, so you don't have to type it each time.

Most graphical FTP clients looks pretty much like Windows Explorer, except that the FTP client has two panes: one for your local machine and one for the server. Navigate to the appropriate directory (in both panes), and drag files from the local pane to the server pane. That's it! Figure 3-2 shows a sample screen in LeapFTP. Other graphical FTP clients work basically the same way.

The directory structure of a Web server can be incredibly complex, but most hosting services allow users access only to the directories they need for their work. On Unix servers, the directory in which Web files are stored is usually called htdocs. If you have a basic end-user hosting account, you probably don't have access to any directories above this one, so you needn't worry about finding the right directory. You can create your own directory structure within your user directory if desired.

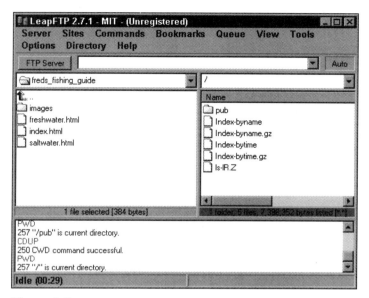

Figure 3-2
*Using LeapFTP to transfer files to and from a Web server. The window pane
on the left shows the local machine, and the pane on the right shows the
server.*

The Web-Editing Process

Here is a step-by-step explanation of the process by which a Web page is created
(or changed) and made available on a Web server:

1. Using your chosen Web editor, create a new HTML file, or open an exist-
    ing one (any of the HTML files on the CD-ROM will do for an example).

2. Make the desired edits to the file.

3. Save the file.

4. Open the file using a Web browser.

5. Examine the page in the browser. If it looks acceptable, proceed to the
    next step. If not, return to your Web editor and make corrections.

6. Launch your FTP client.

7. Enter the necessary information to connect to your Web server: address, user name, and password. Instruct the FTP client to connect to the Web server.

8. Using your FTP client, navigate to the appropriate directory, and upload the HTML file to the server.

9. Return to your Web browser, and open the live file (the copy on the server, not the copy on your local machine).

10. Examine the page live on the Web. If it looks okay, congratulations! You're done.

Done!

REVIEW

In this session, you have learned that a Web site consists of a group of files stored on a Web server. You have also learned:

- The steps required to establish a Web presence
- How to understand a URL
- How to transfer files to your Web server

QUIZ YOURSELF

1. What makes a collection of computer files a Web site? (See "Making Information Available Worldwide.")

2. What is the difference between an Internet-access account and a Web-hosting account? (See "Web-Hosting Services.")

3. What is a URL, and what information does it contain? (See "Understanding URLs.")

4. What is a domain name? (See "About Domain Names.")

5. What protocol is used to transfer files between a local computer and a Web server? What type of software does this require? (See "Exchanging Files with Your Web Server.")

Creating Hyperlinks Using the Anchor Tag

Session Checklist

✔ Using the Anchor tag to create hyperlinks

✔ Using hyperlinks in a Web page

✔ Organizing pages into a Web site

**30 Min.
To Go**

You have learned that a Web page is based on an HTML file, which is really just a plain text file. But how can a mere text file deliver graphics, anima-tion, audio, and all the other things that bring the Web to life? The answer is *links*.

Text content is included directly within an HTML file, as you've seen. All other types of data are accessed through links, which connect the HTML file with other files (which may be almost any type of file) also on a Web server. But perhaps the most interesting link of all, and the one that gives the World Wide Web its name, is the Anchor tag.

Using the Anchor tag, you can create a *hyperlink* from an HTML file to another HTML file or to another point in the same file. This link is visible on the Web page, and when viewers click it, they are transported to the new page.

Defining a Text Hyperlink

Hypertext is so called because it is far more than just text. It offers a means to connect various text documents and other files together in endlessly flexible ways. As a helpful analogy, consider a cross-reference in a book. When you see a note that reads "See chapter such-and-such for more information on such-and-such a topic," you have to flip through the pages of the book to find the section referred to. What tedium! What if the cross-reference could take you instantly to the page referred to even if that page were in a completely different book located in a library on another continent? That's what hyperlinks enable you to do.

To a computing person, this is known as *random access*. In other words, you don't have to read a hypertext document from beginning to end but can jump around as you please. In fact, the term "World Wide Web" was coined to describe the dense network of links that connect the millions of sites around the world.

Hyperlinks are easier to demonstrate than to describe, so here's how to create one.

Instead of creating a new HTML file for this and subsequent examples, you may want to open the file you have created in Session 2 (which includes the four necessary basic tags), and add the examples to that document as you go.

1. Open Notepad (Windows), Simple Text (Mac) or whatever you're using as your Web editor.
2. Type the following code (Listing 4-1):

Listing 4-1:

```
<A HREF="http://www.hungryminds.com">This is a hyperlink</A>.

<P>This is ordinary text.
```

3. Save the file as a plain text file, but give it an `.html` extension.
4. Launch your Web browser, and open the file you have just saved. You should see something very similar to Figure 4-1. Note that the sentence "This is a hyperlink" is highlighted compared to the following sentence. You can tell that it's a hyperlink because it's blue and underlined on the screen.

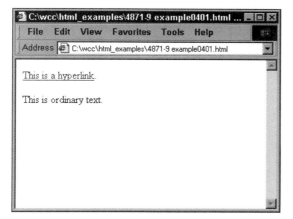

Figure 4-1
The highlighted sentence is a hyperlink. Clicking the hyperlink results in the linked file (in this case, the home page of another Web site) being loaded by the browser.

Most major browsers display hyperlinks by default as blue and underlined. However, the user can change browser settings so that hyperlinks are highlighted in some other way.

5. Place your mouse pointer over the hyperlink and click once. You should now be taken to Hungry Minds' Web site, figuratively speaking. Literally, your browser is loading the page that corresponds to the URL we've listed in our Anchor tag, which is the URL of Hungry Minds' home page. Note that you must be connected to the Internet for this to happen; otherwise, your browser tells you it can't find the requested page.

6. Choose the Back button on your browser to return to the previous page.

Most browsers have keyboard equivalents for many commands, in case you don't choose to use the mouse. For example, in Internet Explorer 5.0 or Netscape 6.0, the Tab key cycles through every hyperlink on a page, highlighting each in turn. Choosing the Enter key loads the highlighted link.

**20 Min.
To Go**

Including Hyperlinks in a Page

To learn the finer points of using the Anchor tag, add a hyperlink to the sample page we have created in Session 2 (in this and following examples, the HTML, HEAD and BODY tags are omitted for brevity).

```
<H3><A HREF="http://www.hungryminds.com/">Hungry Minds
Presents</A>:</H3>

<H1>Freddy's Fishing Guide</H1>

<H2>Saltwater Fishing</H2>

<P>The oceans offer an endless variety of game species, from
inshore favorites to offshore tackle-busters.

    <H2>Freshwater Fishing</H2>

<P>Some of the most avidly pursued fish swim in fresh water, from
the majestic trout and salmon of northern waters to the wily
largemouth bass.
```

We've enclosed the line "Hungry Minds Presents" between a pair of Anchor (A) tags, making it a hyperlink. Take a close look at this bit of code, and note the following details:

- The Anchor element must have both an opening and a closing tag.
- To create a hyperlink, the opening Anchor tag must contain the HREF attribute and must be in this form:

  ```
  <A HREF="reference.html">
  ```

- The part between the quotation marks (don't forget these) is called the reference of the link. It can be any file a Web browser can display, but it must be a valid URL.
- The Anchor tag can be used with any formatting tag, such as the H3 tag in this example. However, any time you use two or more pairs of tags together, they must be nested properly, never overlapped; for example:

  Wrong:

  ```
  <H3><A HREF="http://www.hungryminds.com/">Hungry Minds
  Presents</H3></A>
  ```

Correct:

```
<A HREF="http://www.hungryminds.com/"><H3>Hungry Minds
Presents</H3></A>
```

Best:

```
<H3><A HREF="http://www.hungryminds.com/">Hungry Minds
Presents</A>:</H3>
```

- Never leave a space (or a line break) between the A tag and the beginning or ending of the hyperlinked text. Doing so causes some browsers to display an unsightly "tick" next to the text.

Wrong:

```
<A HREF="http://www.hungryminds.com/">Hungry Minds Presents
</A>
```

Correct:

```
<A HREF="http://www.hungryminds.com/">Hungry Minds Presents</A>
```

- Although punctuation marks can be included in hyperlinked text, it's generally considered bad style to do so. Links appear neater and more attractive when the highlighting (underline) stops short of the punctuation mark.

Bad Style:

```
<A HREF="http://www.hungryminds.com/">Hungry Minds
Presents:</A>
```

Best:

```
<A HREF="http://www.hungryminds.com/">Hungry Minds
Presents</A>:
```

Hyperlinks are very important, so take the time to learn to code them correctly. Listing 4-2 gives examples of some common errors, and Figure 4-2 shows what the resulting Web page looks like.

Please note that the Web page shown in Figure 4-2 and any other Web site with the Hungry Minds name is created for the purpose of this book, and is not an actual Web site by Hungry Minds.

Listing 4-2:

```
<P>Wrong:
<P><A HREF="http://www.hungryminds.com/">Hungry Minds  </A> is the
publisher of this book.
```

Continued

Listing 4-2 *(continued)*

```
<P>Correct:
<P><A HREF="http://www.hungryminds.com/">Hungry Minds</A> is the
publisher of this book.

<P>Bad Style:
<A HREF="http://www.hungryminds.com/">Hungry Minds Presents:</A>

<P>Best:
<A HREF="http://www.hungryminds.com/">Hungry Minds Presents</A>:
```

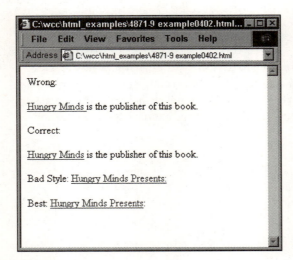

Figure 4-2
An example page in Internet Explorer, showing various sloppily coded hyperlinks. Not all browsers yield the same results, but get in the habit of coding links correctly to avoid any potential problems.

**10 Min.
To Go**

Organizing Pages into a Web Site

A hyperlink can refer to:

- A separate Web site.
- Another page within the same site.
- A specific location within the same page or another page.

Linking to a page within the same site

In the previous example, we have created an *off-site link* (that is, a hyperlink to another Web site). Now we'll create a link to another page on our site. But first we need another page to link to. Add two more pages to our site as follows:

1. If you haven't already, create a directory for our sample site, and save the example page you created in Listing 2-1 as `index.html`. This is the home page of our site.

2. Save the same file as `freshwater.html` and again as `saltwater.html`. We now have two more HTML files, each of which we'll modify to create two section hubs for our site. Using an existing HTML file as the template for a new file is a good practice, as it can save you a lot of typing as well as ensure that your pages are consistent.

3. Now open `index.html` and modify the code as shown in Listing 4-3. This creates two hyperlinks that point to the two pages we've just created:

Listing 4-3:

```
<H3><A HREF="http://www.hungryminds.com/">Hungry Minds
Presents</A>:</H3>
<H1>Freddy's Fishing Guide</H1>

<H2>
<A HREF="saltwater.html">Saltwater Fishing</A>
</H2>

<P>The oceans offer an endless variety of game species, from
inshore favorites to offshore tackle-busters.

<H2>
<A HREF="freshwater.html">Freshwater Fishing</A>
</H2>

<P>Some of the most avidly pursued fish swim in fresh water,
from the majestic trout and salmon of northern waters to the
wily largemouth bass.
```

4. Save `index.html`; then load it in your Web browser. The two section headings should now appear as hyperlinks. When you click them, they should load their two respective section hub pages: saltwater and freshwater. For this to work, all three HTML files must be in the same directory.

Congratulations! You've created a Web site.

Linking to a location within a page

Sometimes you may wish to create a hyperlink that points to a specific location within a Web page, especially if it's a long page. To do so, you need to learn to use another attribute of the A tag: the NAME attribute. Consider this example:

```
<A NAME="location">Text</A>
```

This Anchor tag is like the ones you have learned to use earlier in this session, except that it does not have an HREF attribute, so it does not create a hyperlink. Instead, it gives a name to a location on a Web page, so that a hyperlink elsewhere in the same or another HTML document can refer to this location by name.

A NAME Anchor is invisible on a Web page. The text it wraps around is not affected in any way. Certain browsers may not be able to find the NAME Anchor if it's empty, however, so always wrap a NAME Anchor around some text.

Now add some content to your Web site, learning to use NAME Anchors in the process:

1. Open `freshwater.html`. You have created this file by using `index.html` as a template, so at this point the two files should be identical, except for any changes you may have made in the previous editing session.

2. This page is dedicated to freshwater fish (you'll probably want to substitute some of your own content for my fishy example). Change the TITLE tag as follows:

   ```
   <TITLE>Freshwater Fish - Freddy's Fishing Guide</TITLE>
   ```

   Do not change the HTML, HEAD or BODY tags.

3. Change the content of the BODY section as follows (Listing 4-4):

Listing 4-4:

```
<H3><A HREF="index.html">Freddy's Fishing Guide</A></H3>
<H1>Freshwater Fish</H1>
```

```
<H2>
Northern Species
</H2>

<P><A NAME="salmon">Salmon</A> and Trout are the royalty of the
fishing world, and many are the elegantly turned-out anglers
who pursue these majestic fish with the fly rod.

<P>Those who prefer a dangerous edge to their fishing adventure
may choose to pursue the toothy Pike and Muskellunge.

<H2>
Southern Species
</H2>

<P><A NAME="bass">The wily Largemouth Bass</A> is a favorite of
anglers throughout the United States. A wide variety of
artificial lures is effective against these hard-fighting
predators.

<P>The Smallmouth Bass differs little in appearance from the
Largemouth, but tends to have different habits, often requiring
a different choice of tackle or bait.
```

4. You have added two NAME Anchors: one at the word "Salmon," and one at the words "The wily Largemouth Bass." When used with the NAME attribute, the Anchor tag does not affect the appearance of the page in any way, so it doesn't matter exactly what bit of text it is wrapped around.

5. The NAME Anchor by itself does not create a hyperlink. It creates only a named location, or *handle*, that a hyperlink can refer to. To create a link to such a handle, use the file name followed by the Pound sign (#) followed by the handle. Open index.html and modify it as follows:

```
<H3><A HREF="http://www.hungryminds.com/">Hungry Minds
Presents</A>:</H3>
```

```
<H1>Freddy's Fishing Guide</H1>

<H2><A HREF="saltwater.html">Saltwater Fishing</A></H2>

<P>The oceans offer an endless variety of game species, from
inshore favorites to offshore tackle-busters.

<H2><A HREF="freshwater.html">Freshwater Fishing</A></H2>

<P>Some of the most avidly pursued fish swim in fresh water,
from the majestic <A HREF="freshwater.html#salmon">trout and
salmon</A> of northern waters to the wily <A
HREF="freshwater.html#bass">largemouth bass</A>.
```

6. You have created two links to two different locations within the file
    `freshwater.html`. A HREF="freshwater.html#salmon creates a link to
    the location named salmon, and A HREF="freshwater.html#bass cre-
    ates a link to the location named bass. Save both `freshwater.html` and
    `index.html` and load `index.html` into your Web browser. This page
    should now look something like Figure 4-3. Test the first link by clicking
    "trout and salmon." You should be taken to the location within `freshwa-`
    `ter.html` where the salmonoids are mentioned.

7. You may have noticed another small change to `freshwater.html`. The
    intro line at the top is now a link to `index.html`, the home page of the
    site. Click this link to return to the home page. Of course, you can return
    to the home page by choosing the Back button on your browser, but it is
    good form to include a link to the home page on every page of a site.

8. Now test the second link by clicking "Bass." You should be taken to the
    paragraph in `freshwater.html` that discusses Bass, as shown in
    Figure 4-4.

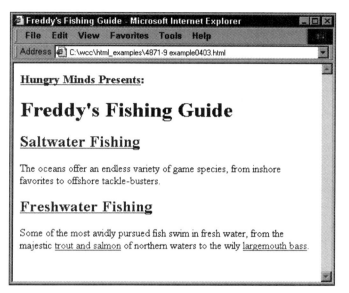

Figure 4-3
Our home page now contains five hyperlinks. One is an off-site link to Hungry Minds' Web site, and two are links to the main hub pages of our site, freshwater and saltwater. The two links embedded in the paragraph text are links to specific locations within the freshwater page.

Because the pages in this example are very short, with only a little text, it may be hard to see the point of links such as these. But they are very handy in long documents of many paragraphs. NAME Anchors such as these can be used to create a table of contents at the top of a long page, which can make navigating the page much easier.

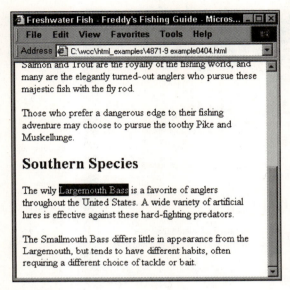

Figure 4-4
Clicking the link to "Bass" loads the freshwater page and scrolls the browser window to the paragraph about Bass.

Done!

REVIEW

In this session, you have begun working with hyperlinks. This has included:

- Creating a text hyperlink by using the Anchor (A) tag.
- Incorporating hyperlinks into a Web page.
- Organizing pages into an interlinked site.

QUIZ YOURSELF

1. What tag is used to create a hyperlink? (See "Defining a Text Hyperlink.")
2. What attribute must this tag contain to create a hyperlink? (See "Defining a Text Hyperlink.")

3. Why should a hyperlink never begin or end with a space or line break? (See "Including Hyperlinks in a Page.")

4. What are three things a hyperlink can refer to? (See "Organizing Pages into a Web Site.")

5. How can you create a named location within a Web page that can be referred to by a hyperlink? (See "Linking to a Location within a Page.")

PART

I

Friday Evening

1. What language is used to build Web pages?

2. You can create and view a Web page with just two software tools. What are these?

3. An HTML file can be viewed or edited. What's the difference?

4. What are three kinds of Web-editing software tools?

5. For the beginning designer, which type of editor is best, and why?

6. What does the Head section of an HTML document contain?

7. What does the Body section of an HTML document contain?

8. What tags can you use to create a set of four line breaks in an HTML document?

9. What's the standard way to set off a new paragraph in an HTML document? What tag can you use to create this effect?

10. If a Paragraph tag directly follows a Heading tag, how many line breaks result?

11. A Web site is a collection of computer files, but what makes it a Web site?

12. Internet Service Providers (ISPs) offer two types of service: Internet access and Web hosting. What's the difference?

13. What information is in a URL?

14. What is a domain name?

15. What software tool is used to transfer files to and from a Web server?

16. What tag do you use to define a hyperlink?

17. Which attribute of the Anchor tag defines the destination of a hyperlink?

18. Why shouldn't you begin or end hyperlinked text with a space or line break?

19. A hyperlink can refer to various types of destination files. Name three.

20. How do you define a named location within a file that can be referred to by a hyperlink?

☑ Friday

☑ **Saturday**

☐ Sunday

PART

II

Saturday
Morning

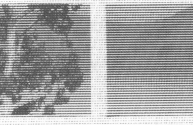

Using Text-Formatting Tags

Session Checklist

✔	Using style tags and lists to make text stand out
✔	Using special characters
✔	Understanding tag attributes

**30 Min.
To Go**

ou already know how to make text appear bold by applying the B tag. The B tag is just one of many tags that can be used to apply various special effects to text.

Applying Text Styles

Type the following code example; then view it in your browser. Listing 5-1 shows the code for various text-styling tags, and Figure 5-1 shows the resulting Web page.

Listing 5-1:

```
<P><B>This is bold text.</B>

<P><STRONG>The STRONG tag has the same effect as the B
tag.</STRONG>
```

Continued

Listing 5-1 *(continued)*

```
<P><I>This is italic text.</I>

<P><EM>The EM (Emphasis) tag has the same effect as the I tag.</EM>

<P><B><I>This is bold italic text.</I></B> Be sure to nest tags
<B><I>correctly</I></B>.

<P><U>Underlined text is not recommended.</U>

<P>Special tags include SUP (superscript) and SUB (subscript).
For example:

<P>E=mc<SUP>2</SUP>

<P>H<SUB>2</SUB>O
```

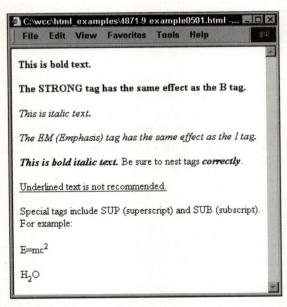

Figure 5-1
These are only a few of the ways text can be styled using HTML tags.

To add more tags to your HTML vocabulary, consult a good HTML reference, such as those listed in Appendix C on the companion CD-ROM. An HTML reference can also help you remember which tags require closing tags and which don't, and what possible attributes each tag may have.

This example is mostly self-explanatory, but take note of two points:

1. Just because you can do something doesn't mean you should. Excessive use of text effects is one of the marks of an amateur site. Consult a style guide to learn accepted usage of bold and italic text. The Chicago Manual of Style is one of the most popular style guides. Learn more about it at: http://www.press.uchicago.edu/Misc/Chicago/cmosfaq.html.

2. Generally, the Underline (U) tag should not be used. It's traditional to display hyperlinks as underlined text, so text treated with the U tag may be mistaken for a hyperlink.

Creating Lists by Using the OL and UL Tags

Bulleted lists can make text easier to read and can aid comprehension by making relationships among topics stand out clearly. HTML provides several types of lists. You can create an ordered list by using the Ordered List (OL) and List Item (LI) tags. The OL tag begins a list and must have a companion closing OL tag at the end of the list. The LI tag specifies the beginning of each item on the list. It has an optional closing tag.

```
<P>Steps to establishing a Web presence:

<OL>
<LI>Establish a hosting account at an ISP.</LI>
<LI>Register a domain name, or arrange to use an existing one.
</LI>
<LI>Have your ISP set up your domain in their DNS.</LI>
</OL>
```

The Unordered List (UL) tag works exactly the same way, except that a "bullet" instead of a number sets off each list item (Listing 5-2).

Listing 5-2:

```
<P>Popular freshwater fish:

<UL>

<LI>Salmonids
     <UL>
          <LI>Salmon
          <LI>Trout
     </UL>

<LI>Bass
     <UL>
          <LI>Largemouth Bass
          <LI>Smallmouth Bass
     </UL>

<LI>Carp and other rough fish
</UL>
```

Note that lists can be nested inside of lists, as in Listing 5-2, by including a list element (OL or UL) within an individual list item (LI). Whenever you nest one element inside another, it's customary to indent the code an additional level for clarity. Note also that this time we have dispensed with the optional closing LI tag. Figure 5-2 shows what these lists look like in a Web browser.

Using Character-Entity References

A *character entity reference* is another type of element that you can use in an HTML document. It isn't a tag, but rather a stand-alone element that has a couple of different uses.

20 Min. To Go

Taking advantage of the extended character set

What if you need to use characters that aren't on your computer keyboard? A wide range of characters and symbols is in the *extended character set*. Some of these characters are variants of letters of the alphabet, such as the *e* with an acute accent used in words such as *café* and *résumé*. The international nature of the Web means that this situation comes up often, as many foreign languages require such characters. Other special characters include common symbols such as the Copyright (©) and Trademark (™) symbols.

With today's computer operating systems, using the extended character set is no problem. Windows users can use the Character Map (Choose Start ⇨ Programs ⇨ Accessories ⇨ System Tools ⇨ Character Map) to find any desired character and can copy and paste it into any text application. Each character also has an identifying number that can be used with the Alt key to insert the character (for example, Alt+0233 inserts an *e* with an acute accent).

Figure 5-2
The Netscape browser renders ordered and unordered lists.

However, because the Web is worldwide and designed to be accessible using any computer platform, we can't assume that everyone has access to all characters or even that everyone's browser can display them correctly. Therefore, HTML provides a way to represent characters indirectly by using a character-entity reference. Representing special characters this way increases the likelihood that they will be displayed as intended in unusual browsers. For example, the *e* acute can be represented by:

é

or by:

é

Note three things:

1. A character-entity reference always begins with an ampersand (&) and ends with a semicolon (;).

2. You can refer to the desired character using its number in the character set (the same number used to refer to it in any text application) preceded by the Pound (#) sign. *Some* characters also have easy-to-remember names you can use instead of the number.

3. Unlike tags, entity references must be in lowercase.

Type the following code (Listing 5-3) into your editor, and view it in your browser. We've expressed the special characters ñ and é three ways: using the numeric reference, using the name reference, and including the character directly in the HTML code. Most browsers display all three correctly, as shown in Figure 5-3. To avoid any potential problems, however, use character-entity references for characters from the extended character set.

Listing 5-3:

```
<P>Espa&#241;ol
<P>Espa&ntilde;ol
<P>Español
<P>Caf&eacute;s, Caf&#233;s and more Cafés.
```

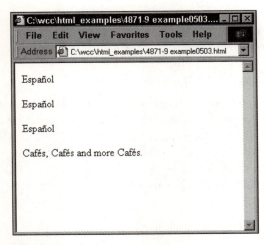

Figure 5-3
Internet Explorer 5.0 displays all these examples correctly. Some users' systems may not, however; to be on the safe side, use character-entity references.

Using special characters

Certain characters cannot be included in HTML body text because they have special meanings in HTML code. Obviously, the left-angle bracket and right-angle bracket (< and >, respectively) fit into this category. If you need to use an angle bracket in your text, you *must* refer to it by its character-entity reference. This is often done when presenting examples of HTML code. For example, suppose you are creating an online HTML tutorial and want to give an example of how to use the BR tag:

```
Use the <BR> tag to create line breaks, as in this example:
<BR>First line
<BR>Second line
<BR>Third line
```

This code, of course, causes actual line breaks for each occurrence of the BR tag. The tags themselves are not displayed on screen, and the code does not serve its purpose of providing an example.

To achieve the desired result, replace the angle brackets with their character-entity references (Listing 5-4):

Listing 5-4:

```
Use the &lt;BR&gt; tag to create line breaks, as in this example:
&lt;BR&gt;First line
&lt;BR&gt;Second line
&lt;BR&gt;Third line
```

Figure 5-4 shows that the angle brackets are displayed in the Web page as desired.

The ampersand and double quote signs are also considered special characters and can be expressed by & and ", respectively. Unlike the angle brackets, most browsers display these two symbols even if they are used directly.

You may sometimes find it necessary to refer to a comprehensive listing of all the possible special characters. The Web Design Group's HTML Help site (http://www.htmlhelp.com/**) includes listings of the various extended character sets.**

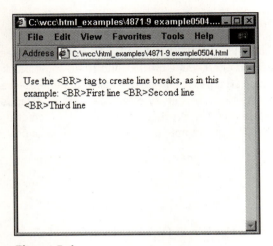

Figure 5-4
To display angle brackets in a Web page, their character-entity references must be used in the HTML code.

Inserting spaces by using the non-breaking space entity

The non-breaking space entity ( ) has two uses:

1. *Creating multiple spaces.* You have learned in Session 2 that the browser ignores more than one space in HTML code. If you need to insert multiple spaces in text for any reason, the   entity is a handy way to do it. For example, some designers simply can't get used to the double line break generally used to set off a new paragraph in Web documents. If you insist on using the more traditional method of indenting the first line, you can do it by using the BR tag and the   entity, as shown in Listing 5-5. Figure 5-5 shows the result.

Listing 5-5:

```
       
The wily Largemouth Bass is a favorite of anglers throughout
the United States. A wide variety of artificial lures is
effective against these hard-fighting predators. Try a plastic
worm, jig or crankbait.

<BR>
```

```
       
```

The Smallmouth Bass differs little in appearance from the
Largemouth, but tends to have different habits, often requiring
a different choice of tackle or bait.

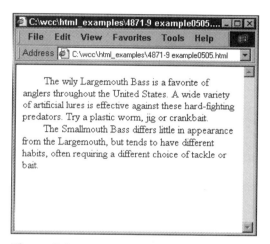

Figure 5-5
Print-style indents can be created by using the BR tag and   entity.

2. *Preventing a line break.* Normally, text on a Web page automatically
    wraps (that is, a line break is inserted) at whatever point is appropriate,
    depending on the width of the browser window. If you have certain words
    (for example, in a heading) you do not want broken up by a line break,
    insert a   between them; they'll stick together through thick
    and thin.

More Handy Formatting Tags

**10 Min.
To Go**

HTML provides a vast array of tags you can use to structure your documents.
I recommend consulting an HTML reference to learn about other tags that you
may find useful. Here we have just enough space to discuss a few of the more
unique ones.

Creating indents by using the BLOCKQUOTE tag

You can use the BLOCKQUOTE tag to indent entire sections of text, as in Listing 5-6. Figure 5-6 shows the resulting page.

Listing 5-6:

```
<P>The wily Largemouth Bass is a favorite of anglers throughout
the United States. A wide variety of artificial lures is effective
against these hard-fighting predators. Try a plastic worm, jig or
crankbait. Here's a quote from an anonymous angler:

<BLOCKQUOTE>
<P>Those bass are really something. One day me and my brother
caught twenty bass before breakfast. The biggest one was ten
pounds, blah blah blah, etc. etc. etc.
</BLOCKQUOTE>

<P>The Smallmouth Bass differs little in appearance from the
Largemouth, but tends to have different habits, often requiring a
different choice of tackle or bait.
```

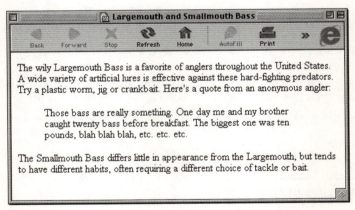

Figure 5-6
Indenting a block of text by using the BLOCKQUOTE tag.

Using the PRE tag for special formatting

Although HTML provides many ways to format text, it's not always possible to line text elements up as precisely as you would like them. For times when you simply must preserve the exact positioning of a passage of text, the PRE tag is like a secret weapon. Everything between PRE tags is formatted exactly as it is in the code.

PRE is handy for displaying examples of computer code. As you have learned in Session 2, good coding practice dictates that you use indents and line breaks to make code more readable. An online coding tutorial might present an example such as Listing 5-7:

Listing 5-7:

```
<PRE>
    A code example.

            Always indent your code in a logical way.
                This makes it easier to read and to edit.
                It also makes the relationships among elements clear.

    The end of the code example.
</PRE>
```

Figure 5-7 shows how this text appears on the Web page, retaining its line breaks and indents. It would have been very complex to create this formatting any other way.

Don't overuse the PRE tag. HTML provides much more powerful tools for positioning elements on a page: tables (which you'll learn about in Session 12) and CSS (which you'll learn about in Session 19). In certain situations, however, the PRE tag can be very handy.

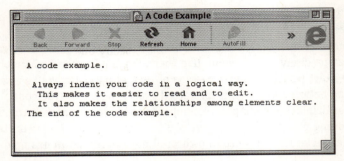

Figure 5-7
The PRE tag lets you format text directly.

The HR Tag: Introducing Tag Attributes

The Horizontal Rule (HR) tag is easy to understand. A stand-alone tag (it has no corresponding closing tag), it inserts a horizontal line at the desired location. You can use it to separate sections of text, as in this example:

```
<P>Section of text

<HR>

<P>Another section of text
```

The HR tag is easy to overuse. Most designers favor using white space, not horizontal rules, to separate sections. But used in just the right place, a horizontal rule can look great. Because the HR tag in its plain form is rather dull, let's use it as an example to introduce an important concept that has to do with tags: *attributes*.

Some tags allow you to modify their effects by including one or more optional attributes. An attribute lets you specify a certain value to fine-tune the effect of a tag. Each tag can take certain attributes, and you can specify one or more of these for a particular tag (a few tags, such as the Anchor tag, are useless without at least one attribute). As an example, add some optional attributes to the HR tag:

```
<P>Section of text

<HR SIZE="4" WIDTH="50%" NOSHADE>

<P>Another section of text
```

Here we have added three attributes to the HR tag to change the default attributes of the horizontal rule. The attributes are separated by spaces, and they may appear in any order. Some attributes take a value (SIZE, WIDTH), and some don't (NOSHADE). The value (technically called an *argument*) of an attribute should always be set off by quotation marks and connected to the attribute name by an equal sign, just as you have learned to use the HREF attribute of the A tag in Session 4. Consult an HTML reference to see what attributes are allowed for any particular tag, and what range of values each attribute can take.

What happens if you specify no attributes for a tag? It depends on the tag. The HR tag has default values, which we have changed in this example:

- The default size for an HR is 2 *pixels* (a pixel is a single point in an image. Many size values in HTML are specified in pixels). Here we've fattened up the horizontal rule a bit by specifying a size of 4 pixels.
- The default width for an HR is 100%. Here we have specified 50, so the rule is only half the width of the page.
- By default, a horizontal rule has a two-toned, 3D look. By specifying the NOSHADE attribute, we eliminate this and make it a solid line instead.

Figure 5-8 shows what the modified horizontal rule looks like. The HR tag is probably one you won't use that often. Attributes, however, are very important; you'll use them a lot in the next session, so be sure to understand how they work.

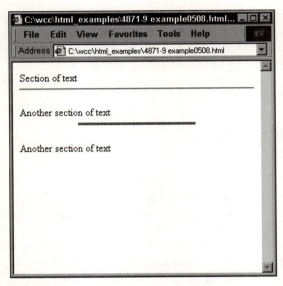

Figure 5-8
The top horizontal rule has the tag's default values. The bottom one has been modified by specifying values for its optional attributes.

Done!

REVIEW

In this session, you have learned several more ways to format text:

- Applying text styles and creating lists
- Using character entities
- Creating horizontal rules with the HR tag

Also, you have learned about optional attributes, which can refine the effects of tags.

QUIZ YOURSELF

1. What are two alternative tags you can use to create bold text? Italic text? (See "Applying Text Styles.")

2. Why do most Web designers not use underlined text as a means of emphasis? (See "Applying Text Styles.")

3. What two tags are required to create an ordered list? (See "Creating Lists by Using the OL and UL Tags.")

4. How can you display angle brackets in a Web page? (See "Using Special Characters.")

5. What is an attribute? (See "The HR Tag: Introducing Tag Attributes.")

6

Setting Font Attributes

Session Checklist

✔ Specifying a typeface

✔ Sizing text by using the FONT tag

✔ Specifying colors

**30 Min.
To Go**

Y ou've learned to add styles such as bold and italic to your text and to control the position of text on a page in various ways. However, to make your text really attractive and to give your site an individual look and feel, you need a way to select particular font faces and to control text characteristics such as size and color.

Using the FONT Tag

The simplest way to achieve this, although not necessarily the correct way, is by using the FONT tag. The FONT tag is officially *deprecated* by the *World Wide Web Consortium* (W3C), which means that it's considered obsolete and may not be supported in future versions of HTML. I don't recommend its use except as a learning tool. The preferred way to set font characteristics is by using Cascading Style Sheets (CSS), as you learn in Session 17. However, a lot of existing sites do use the FONT element, and its attributes are similar to those used by CSS, so it's good to know how the FONT element works.

 The *World Wide Web Consortium* (W3C) sets standards for HTML and other Web languages. Their Web site (http://www.w3.org/**) is considered the authority on what is or isn't correct HTML.**

 The issues of deprecated and non-standard tags are explained in Appendix D on the companion CD-ROM.

The FONT tag allows several possible attributes; we discuss three: FACE, SIZE and COLOR. You can use one or more of these attributes (a FONT tag with no attributes at all is pointless) in a single FONT tag. In Listing 6-1, we use the FONT tag to specify red text in the Arial typeface. Figure 6-1 shows the result.

Listing 6-1:

```
<FONT FACE="Arial" SIZE="2" COLOR="red">Red arial type.</FONT>
<P>Regular old black type.
```

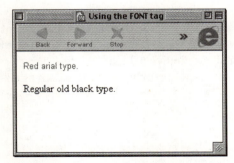

Figure 6-1
The first line uses the font face, size, and color defined in the FONT tag.
If these values are not specified, text is displayed according to the browser's
default values, as the second line of text shows.

Specifying a Typeface

You can specify any font (typeface) you like in the FACE attribute, but the desired font is displayed only if it is present on the user's system. If the specified font isn't found, the default browser font is displayed. Of course, there's no way to know what fonts any particular user may or may not have, and the font the browser chooses as a substitute may be quite different from the one you intend. To deal with this problem, you can specify a priority list of desired fonts. If the first font on the list is present, it is used. If not, the second on the list appears, and so on. For example:

```
<FONT FACE="Verdana, Arial, sans-serif" SIZE="2" COLOR="red">Red
arial type.</FONT>
```

In the preceding example, if the font Verdana is present on the user's system, it is used. If Verdana is not present, the browser attempts to use Arial (a more common font). If Arial is not available, the browser chooses any available font from the sans-serif family.

Fonts may be classified into families that share certain basic characteristics. The most common fonts may be defined as either *serif* or *sans-serif*. A serif is a tiny line that decorates the end of the main stroke of a letter. Fonts that have serifs are referred to as serif, and fonts without serifs are called sans-serif.

This is a serif font.
This is a sans-serif font.

In print, it is traditional to use a serif font for main body text and to use sans-serif fonts for headings and sometimes for other elements such as sidebars. On the Web, however, it's common to use a sans-serif font for body text. Some designers feel that sans-serif fonts are easier to read on screen. The choice is up to you.

Other font families HTML recognizes include *monospace* (often used for code examples) and *cursive* (fonts that emulate handwriting).

The usual form for a font-face priority list is:

```
FACE="Desired Font, Generic Windows Font, Generic Mac Font,
Font Family"
```

**20 Min.
To Go**

Many fonts are available, but most users have only a few installed on their systems. There is really little point in specifying an obscure font face, for it is seen as intended by only a tiny fraction of Web users. If you must use a specialty font for a certain bit of text such as a heading, you can always use a graphic for the heading instead of straight HTML text, although this approach has its own drawbacks.

You learn to add graphics to your pages in Session 7.

It's best to specify only fairly common font faces that you can be sure a fair number of users have. But this doesn't mean limiting yourself to two or three fonts. A good compromise is to limit yourself to the dozen or so TrueType fonts that come with Windows. A large percentage of users have these fonts available. Inevitably, however, some do not, so specify a very common font as a second choice (such as the serif font Times or the sans-serif font Arial).

Another little problem arises from the fact that the Windows and Mac operating systems often use different names for the same fonts. For example, Arial is often called Helvetica in the Mac world. Specify an equivalent Mac font as your third choice and the font family name as your last choice. Now you can be sure that *almost* all users see something at least reasonably similar to the font you want them to see.

In Listing 6-2, we've chosen Verdana, a sans-serif font, for our heading, and Garamond, a serif font, for our body text, together with appropriate alternatives. Note that the FONT tag can be used in conjunction with Heading tags and other text-formatting tags (but remember to nest tags correctly). Figure 6-2 shows the result.

Listing 6-2:

```
<H1><FONT FACE="Verdana, Arial, Helvetica, sans-serif">Freddy's
Fishing Guide</FONT></H1>

<H2><FONT FACE="Verdana, Arial, Helvetica, sans-serif">Saltwater
Fishing</FONT></H2>

<P><FONT FACE="Garamond, Times, serif">The oceans offer an
endless variety of game species, from inshore tasties to offshore
tackle-busters.</FONT>

<H2><FONT FACE="Verdana, Arial, sans-serif">Freshwater
Fishing</FONT></H2>
```

```
<P><FONT FACE="Garamond, Times, serif">Some of the most avidly
pursued fish swim in fresh water, from the majestic trout and
salmon of northern waters to the wily largemouth bass.</FONT>
```

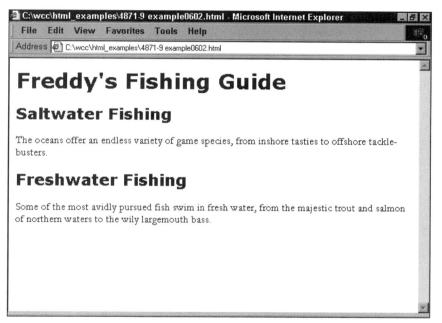

Figure 6-2
Two of Windows' standard fonts, Verdana and Garamond, give users a
welcome break from the ubiquitous Arial and Times.

Setting Type Size

The SIZE attribute of the FONT tag can specify either absolute size or relative size. Possible absolute size values are 1 through 7. If you put a plus (+) or a minus (–) sign before the numeric value, the text is sized the specified number of sizes larger or smaller than the preceding text, as in Listing 6-3. Figure 6-3 shows the resulting Web page.

Listing 6-3:

```
<P><FONT SIZE="7">This is size 7 text. Big!</FONT>

<P><FONT SIZE="1">This is size 1 text. Small!</FONT>

<P><FONT SIZE="3">This is size 3 text. Three is also the default
size.</FONT>

<P><FONT SIZE="+2">This text is two sizes larger than the
preceding text (which makes it size 5).</FONT>
```

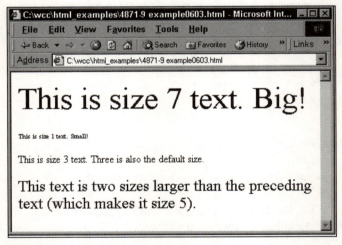

Figure 6-3
Fun with fonts. The FONT tag provides seven possible text sizes that can be specified in absolute or relative terms.

10 Min. To Go

Specifying Colors

HTML enables you to specify the color of almost any element, including text. However, this is one of those effects that should be used with great caution, if at all. Most Web designers agree that setting body text in anything other than black is rarely acceptable and tends to make the text harder to read. One exception is provided by the many sites that use black as a background color, in which case the text should be white or some other light color.

Colored headings, however, can be attractive. Spice up our previous example even further by making the headings blue, in keeping with our aquatic subject matter (Listing 6-4):

Listing 6-4:

```
<H1><FONT COLOR="blue" FACE="Verdana, Arial, Helvetica,
sans-serif">Freddy's Fishing Guide</FONT></H1>

<H2><FONT COLOR="blue" FACE="Verdana, Arial, Helvetica,
sans-serif">Saltwater Fishing</FONT></H2>

<P><FONT FACE="Garamond, Times, serif">The oceans offer an
endless variety of game species, from inshore tasties to offshore
tackle-busters.</FONT>

<H2><FONT COLOR="blue" FACE="Verdana, Arial, sans-
serif">Freshwater Fishing</FONT></H2>

<P><FONT FACE="Garamond, Times, serif">Some of the most avidly
pursued fish swim in fresh water, from the majestic trout and
salmon of northern waters to the wily largemouth bass.</FONT>
```

The most common colors, such as black, white, blue, red, and so on, can be specified directly within a tag (consult an HMTL reference to find out which colors are recognized). However, you are not limited to these colors. By specifying a numeric value, any of over 16 million colors can theoretically be used! I say "theoretically," however, because browsers don't really support that many colors. In Session 10, you learn to use *browser-safe* colors that still give you a wide variety to choose from.

HTML allows you to specify colors for various elements, including backgrounds, table cells, and several other elements explained in later sessions. The code for specifying colors for these elements is the same as the code described here in connection with fonts.

In HTML, a particular color is defined by a string of six characters. This string consists of three two-digit values (in hexadecimal [base 16] notation) that correspond to the Red, Green, and Blue (RGB) values of the color. This can be rather tedious, for although many software applications define colors by their RGB values, most use ordinary base 10 notation, not base 16. You'll need a scientific calculator to make the conversions (Windows users choose Start ⇨ Programs ⇨ Accessories ⇨ Calculator; then choose View ⇨ Scientific). Users of any OS can use the online calculator at `http://www.convertit.com/Go/ConvertIt/ Calculators/Math/Base_Converter.ASP`.

Some examples:

- Pure red has an RGB value of 255,0,0 (maximum red, minimum green, minimum blue). In hex, 255 equals FF, so red is expressed as FF0000.
- Black has an RGB value of 255,255,255, which translates to FFFFFF.
- White has an RGB value of 0,0,0, which translates to 000000.

To learn to convert color values in a graphic software application to HTML color values, follow these steps:

1. Open any graphics editing application (such as Paint, Paint Shop Pro or Photoshop).
2. Open the color selection dialog box (the exact commands vary from one application to another).
3. Select any of the colors shown in the dialog box. The application displays the Red, Green, and Blue values that correspond to this color.
4. Using a scientific calculator, convert each of these three values to hex (the latest versions of popular graphics programs display color values in both base-10 and hex, making this calculation unnecessary). Each hex value consists of two alphanumeric characters.
5. String the three hex values together (no spaces) to form a six-character string.
6. Enter this string, preceded by a pound sign (#) as the value (argument) of the COLOR attribute in a FONT tag. The same procedure applies to any other element that can take an attribute that specifies a color, such as the BODY tag, or the TD tag.
7. The color of the text (or other element) modified by this tag should match the color you chose in your graphics application.

To return to our example page, if you think the pure blue specified is a little too light, you can specify a deeper ocean blue instead by changing the appropriate FONT tags as follows:

```
<H1><FONT COLOR="#000080" FACE="Verdana, Arial, Helvetica,
sans-serif">Freddy's Fishing Guide</FONT></H1>
```

We have replaced the color value blue with the specific hex value 000080, which is the equivalent of RGB value 0,0,128. Remember that the specific number value must be preceded by the pound sign (#).

What's Wrong with the FONT Tag?

The FONT tag may seem powerful, but it has a couple of serious drawbacks, which is why the best designers don't use it:

- It offers only seven possible type sizes and doesn't let you specify type size in points, which is the standard way of doing so in the publishing world.
- Every text element must have its own FONT tag, as in the previous example. This requires a lot of tedious, repetitive coding and increases the potential for errors. Making a global change to any text element (for example, changing all the headings from blue to red) means changing every FONT tag in a document.

As you've probably guessed by now, there is a much more powerful set of tools available for specifying the attributes of text. These tools are called CSS and are explained more fully in Session 17.

Done!

REVIEW

In this session, you have learned to change the appearance of text by using the FONT tag. This has included:

- Specifying a typeface
- Changing text size
- Setting custom text colors

QUIZ YOURSELF

1. What happens if a typeface specified by a FONT tag is not available on a particular user's system? (See "Specifying a Typeface.")
2. Should body text be set in a serif or sans-serif font? (See "Specifying a Typeface.")

3. What is the effect of including this attribute in a FONT tag: SIZE="-2"?
    (See "Setting Type Size.")

4. What are two ways the color black can be specified within a FONT tag?
    (See "Specifying Colors.")

5. What numeric system does HTML use to specify color values?
    (See "Specifying Colors.")

Session Checklist

✔ Including graphics in a Web page by using the IMG tag

✔ Understanding file addressing

✔ Using attributes of the IMG tag to improve your graphics

***30 Min.
To Go***

As you have learned, text content is included in HTML files directly, whereas other types of media, such as images and sounds, are embedded in a Web page by means of links. You learn to create links to sound files in Session 24. You can create a link to an image file by using the Image (IMG) tag.

Using the IMG Tag to Include Graphics

In Session 4, you learn to use the Anchor tag, which creates an active hyperlink to another Web page or to another location within the same page. The IMG tag also creates a link, in this case to a graphic file. IMG works quite differently from the Anchor tag, however. The IMG tag causes the referenced graphic file to be displayed at a chosen point in a Web page. For example:

```
<IMG SRC="sample_image.gif">
```

This code causes the image file named `sample_image.gif` to be displayed at whatever point on the page the code is inserted. Note these facts about `IMG` tags:

- The `SRC` attribute gives the name of the desired image file. It isn't really optional, as an `IMG` tag with no `SRC` attribute is useless. Like all attributes, it is used with the equal sign (=) and double quotes (").

- Only three graphic formats can be used for Web images: `.gif`, `.jpg`, and `.png`.

 `.png` is a newer file format designed to be an improvement on the older `.gif` and `.jpg` formats. Some older browsers may not support it.

- The specified image file is displayed only if it can be found on the Web server. If a browser is unable to display a requested image file, it displays a broken graphic icon instead, as shown in Figure 7-1.

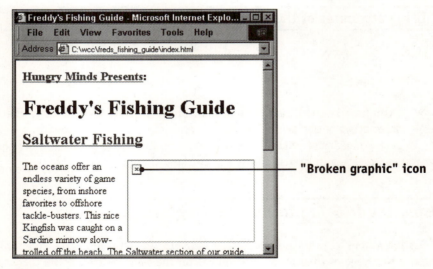

Figure 7-1
A browser may display the broken graphic icon for any of several reasons. To speed page loading, some Web users set their browsers not to display graphics. Sometimes a particular image may simply fail to load because of server overload or some other network bottleneck. Don't let it happen because you have messed up the HTML code!

Absolute versus default addresses

This is a good place to introduce the issue of file addressing. Any time you refer to a file in a tag, as with the A and IMG tags, you can refer to it by an *absolute path* or by a *default path*. An absolute path specifies the full Web address of a file, and a default path specifies only the file's location relative to the Web page that contains the link.

This is an absolute address:

```
http://www.fredsfishingguide.com/images/kingfish.jpg
```

And this is a default address:

```
images/kingfish.jpg
```

To link to a file on another Web site, obviously you must use the absolute address. To link to another file on the same server, you can use an absolute address or a default address. It's better to use default addressing, because it may make the file load a little faster (the browser only has to look for it in the current directory).

There are actually four different file-addressing methods, all of which are explained in Session 20.

When using a default address, be careful that it specifies a valid path from the HTML file with the link to the desired image file. The preceding example works *only* if a file called kingfish.jpg is in a folder called images located *immediately below* the directory containing the file with the link.

Unless you have specific permission from the site owner, never use an absolute address to link to an image on another Web site. Even if you have permission to use the image itself, you are usually expected to copy it to your server and to link only to the local copy. Linking to image files on another site not only increases your page-load time; it amounts to stealing bandwidth from the other site's server.

About file sizes and page-load times

Graphic files present special problems because they are much larger than text files. The larger the file, the longer it takes to load in a user's browser; the more images you use on a page, the longer that page takes to load. It's important to balance the desire for attractive graphics with the need to keep page-load times reasonably short. Excessive page-load times have a definite negative effect on your site's popularity and on the number of return visitors. No one likes to wait, and Web surfers are known for their short attention spans.

In following sessions, you learn several techniques that can help you keep load times down. The most important rule of all, however, is to use graphics sparingly and tastefully. Include only those images that really reinforce your message.

Using IMG Tag Attributes for Better-looking Images

20 Min. To Go

The IMG tag has several optional attributes that can help you optimize the appearance of your graphics. Some of the more important are the WIDTH, HEIGHT, ALT, and BORDER attributes.

The WIDTH and HEIGHT attributes

These two attributes let you specify the size of an image so that the browser can set aside a space for it while continuing to load the rest of the page. Without WIDTH and HEIGHT, the browser must wait to load the entire image before it can load the next text or image element. Thus, proper use of WIDTH and HEIGHT can greatly reduce your apparent page-load times.

WIDTH and HEIGHT should not be used for sizing images but only to list the actual size of an existing image. If you specify values for WIDTH or HEIGHT that are different from the actual width and height of the image, the image will be stretched or squeezed accordingly, but this results in distorted, bad-quality graphics; you should never do things this way. Size your images in a graphic-editing software package as you learn to do in Session 9; then enter the correct WIDTH and HEIGHT values in your HTML code.

Some HTML editors can calculate the correct WIDTH **and** HEIGHT values and insert them into the IMG **tag, so you don't have to remember them or enter them by hand.**

Here's an example IMG tag with WIDTH and HEIGHT attributes correctly used:

```
<IMG SRC="kingfish.jpg" WIDTH="192" HEIGHT="128">
```

The ALT attribute

The ALT attribute enables you to specify a text message that is displayed while the image is loading or if it fails to load. This is very helpful. If a user's system fails to display an image for whatever reason, at least he or she can get an idea of what the image is supposed to convey. It's also a boon to visually disabled people who may not be able to see your image but may be able to read the ALT text or hear it by using a text-to-speech application.

More recent browsers can display the ALT text in a little box when the user holds the mouse over the image. For all these reasons, the ALT attribute should be used with all IMG tags and should contain a brief description of the image, as in this example:

```
<IMG SRC="kingfish.jpg" WIDTH="192" HEIGHT="128" ALT="Picture of a
man holding up a large Kingfish">
```

The BORDER attribute

You can create a black border for an image by including the optional BORDER attribute with a size in pixels. If you don't want a border, it's best to specify BORDER="0". This example displays the image with a border six-pixels wide:

```
<IMG SRC="kingfish.jpg" WIDTH="192" HEIGHT="128" ALT="Picture of a
man holding up a large Kingfish" BORDER="6">
```

Adding an Image Step by Step

Now spruce up our sample home page by adding a picture:

**10 Min.
To Go**

1. Navigate to the directory that contains the sample Web site we've been working on (Windows users choose Start ➪ Programs ➪ Accessories ➪ Windows Explorer), and create a new subdirectory called images. Images can be stored wherever you like, but it's customary to give them their own directory just to keep things organized.

2. Place a .jpg image file in the images directory, and name it kingfish.jpg. If you like, copy this file from the fredsfishingguide/images directory on the CD-ROM. Your directory tree should now look something like the one in Figure 7-2.

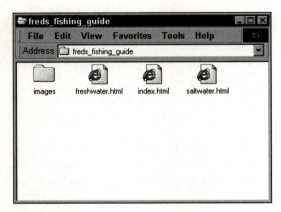

Figure 7-2
Our sample Web site lives in the freds_fishing_guide directory, which so far contains three HTML files and a subdirectory for image files.

The CD-ROM contains both the finished Fred's Fishing Guide Web site (in the `fredsfishingguide` directory) and every numbered listing in every chapter (in the `html examples` directory). For maximum retention of what you learn, I recommend that you type the examples into your Web editor, building a parallel site of your own as you go.

3. Launch your Web editor (word processor or HTML editor), and open the file `index.html` we have created in Session 2 and expanded in Sessions 4, 5 and 6.

4. Take the sample `IMG` tag we have presented earlier in this session, and insert it just under the code for the paragraph on saltwater fishing (Listing 7-1). Place a `P` tag before the `IMG` tag.

Listing 7-1:

```
<H3><A HREF="http://www.hungryminds.com/">Hungry Minds
Presents</A>:</H3>


<H1>Freddy's Fishing Guide</H1>


<H2>Saltwater Fishing</H2>
```

```
<P>The oceans offer an endless variety of game species, from
inshore favorites to offshore tackle-busters.

<P><IMG SRC="images/kingfish.jpg" WIDTH="192" HEIGHT="128"
ALT="Picture of a man holding up a large Kingfish" BORDER="6">

<H2>Freshwater Fishing</H2>

<P>Some of the most avidly pursued fish swim in fresh water,
from the majestic trout and salmon of northern waters to the
wily largemouth bass.
```

5. Figure 7-3 shows the result.

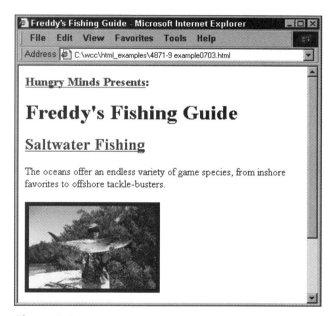

Figure 7-3
*Freddy's home page is looking better and better. A picture truly is worth a
thousand words. It's also worth an extra second or two of page-load time, so
use images sparingly. Note the thick black border we have created by using
the BORDER attribute.*

Done!

REVIEW

In this session, you have learned to include a graphic image in a Web page by using the IMG tag, and you have learned the difference between an absolute path and a default path. Also, you have learned some useful attributes of the IMG tag:

- WIDTH and HEIGHT attributes, which you should always use
- The ALT attribute, also a virtual must
- The optional BORDER attribute

QUIZ YOURSELF

1. What are the three graphic formats that can be used for Web images? (See "Using the IMG Tag to Include Graphics.")

2. When linking to a file within the same site, should you use an absolute or a default address? (See "Absolute versus Default Addresses.")

3. How does using the WIDTH and HEIGHT attributes improve page loading? (See "The WIDTH and HEIGHT Attributes.")

4. What are three reasons why you should always use the ALT attribute in an IMG tag? (See "The ALT Attribute.")

5. What code do you include in an IMG tag if you want the image to be displayed with no border? (See "The BORDER Attribute.")

Combining Graphics and Text

Session Checklist

✔ Creating image hyperlinks

✔ Using an image as a page background

✔ Wrapping text around an image

I n Session 7, you learn to use the IMG tag to insert a graphic into a Web page. Now you can learn some techniques for integrating images smoothly with text and other elements on a page.

**30 Min.
To Go**

Making an Image a Hyperlink

You can make an image a hyperlink just as easily as doing so with text. Simply wrap an Anchor (A) tag around the IMG tag, as in the following example:

```
<P><A HREF="saltwater.html"><IMG SRC="images/kingfish.jpg"
WIDTH="192" HEIGHT="128" ALT="Picture of a Kingfish. Click to go
to the Saltwater page."></A>
```

In Session 7, we add a picture of a Kingfish to our example Fred's Fishing Guide home page. Now we've made that picture a hyperlink leading to the Saltwater hub page. A site user can go to the Saltwater page either by clicking on its text title or on the accompanying image.

 In Session 4, you learn never to leave a space or line break between an Anchor tag and its contents. This applies to images, too. Some browsers display the superfluous space as an unsightly "tick."

You may have noticed that the Anchor tag in the preceding example contains no BORDER attribute. However, in most browsers, this image appears with a narrow, blue border because of the hyperlink. If you don't want a border, you must specify BORDER="0" as in Listing 8-1:

Listing 8-1:

```
<P><A HREF="freshwater.html"><IMG SRC="images/pargo.jpg"
WIDTH="192" HEIGHT="128" ALT="Picture of a Pargo. Click to go to
the Freshwater page." BORDER="0"></A>
```

 For brevity's sake, the code listings in this session contain only the section of code under discussion. The corresponding listings on the companion CD-ROM contain the code for the complete Web page.

Figure 8-1 shows Freddy's home page with two hyperlinked images. The top image has a narrow, blue border, but the bottom image has none.

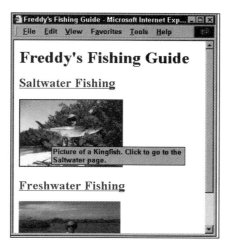

Figure 8-1
The Saltwater and Freshwater sections can each be reached by clicking either a text heading or a picture. Note the use of ALT text to inform the user what happens when he or she clicks the image.

20 Min. To Go

Creating Thumbnail Images

The larger the on-screen size of an image, the larger the image file. That's why the images used in Web pages tend to be small. However, there are times when only a large image can tell the story you need to tell. Fortunately, there's an easy way to set things up so that users who really want to see a large graphic can do so without slowing down the page-load time for everyone else: Create a so-called *teaser* or *thumbnail* image, and link it to the full-size version of the image.

1. Use your graphic editing software to create two versions of the same image: the full-size image and a much smaller version (perhaps 50-pixels wide) called a thumbnail.

2. Place this code (Listing 8-2) in your page (optional tag attributes omitted for clarity):

Listing 8-2:

```
<A HREF="large_image.jpg"><IMG SRC="small_image.jpg" ALT="Click
here to display the full-size image."></A>
```

3. `small_image.jpg` is displayed on the page, as shown in Figure 8-2. When the user moves his or her mouse over this thumbnail image, the ALT text reveals that a larger version is there for the clicking. If the user chooses to click, the larger version is displayed in its own browser window.

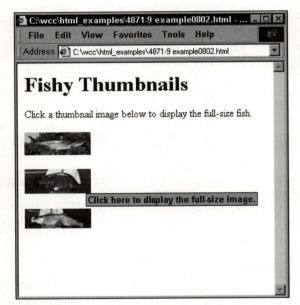

Figure 8-2
Thumbnail images are commonly used to give users a preview of a group of large images without making them wait to load each one.

Until now, we've used the Anchor (A) tag only to link to HTML files. However, an image file (or any other file) can also be the target of an Anchor hyperlink. An image file called by a hyperlink is displayed by itself in its own browser window.

Defining a Background Image

Background images are a subject of controversy among Web designers. Many designers avoid them, as they tend to obscure the foreground text, and add to page-load time. Other designers point out that many people consider them attractive. Everyone seems to agree, however, that a badly designed background is one of the hallmarks of an amateurish site.

To create a background image for a page, simply use the optional BACKGROUND attribute of the BODY tag, as in this example:

```
<BODY BACKGROUND="images/kingfish.jpg">
```

The image kingfish.jpg should appear as the background for the entire page.

Theoretically, any size image can be used. The browser automatically causes the image to *tile* (that is, to repeat itself vertically and horizontally) until it fills up the entire page. There are two approaches to creating a background image. One is to create an image the same size as the intended Web page (for example 640 by 480 pixels). The other is to use a small image (perhaps 20 or 30 pixels square) that creates a pleasing pattern when tiled.

The first approach has a serious drawback. There is no way to know what size window a particular user is using. If the browser window is larger than the background image, it begins to tile, and a little piece of it is visible below it, to the right of it, or both. There's no way to stop this from happening, and most people agree that it looks very bad. For this reason, many designers choose never to use single-image backgrounds. Using a small image that is designed to tile avoids the problem.

The most important rule about using any background image is to make it *very* light in color so that it doesn't obscure the text and distract from the message of the page. Figure 8-3 shows a really objectionable background image, and Figure 8-4 shows a small tiling image used as a background.

Session 22 discusses lightening an image for use as a background.

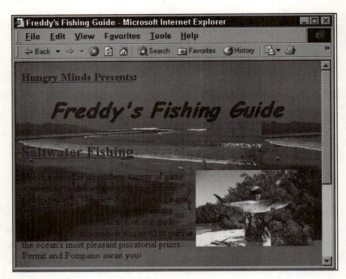

Figure 8-3
This background image is awful. Not only is it much too dark and much too busy, causing it to obscure the page contents; if you look at the right and bottom edges, you can see that it is beginning to tile.

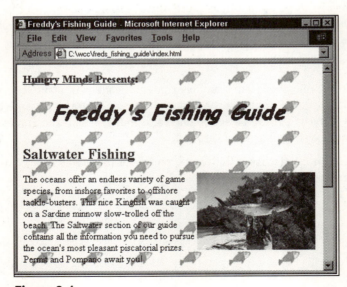

Figure 8-4
Using a very light image designed to tile in a pattern yields much more pleasing results.

Wrapping Text Around Graphics

10 Min. To Go

You can make your pages much more attractive by wrapping text around images. This is done by using the optional ALIGN attribute of the IMG tag. For example, if you include ALIGN="left" in an IMG tag, the image is forced to the left, and the text wraps around it. Open index.html, and modify the code as follows (Listing 8-3):

Listing 8-3:

```
<H3><A HREF="http://www.hungryminds.com/">Hungry Minds
Presents</A>:</H3>

<H1>Freddy's Fishing Guide</H1>

<H2>Saltwater Fishing</H2>

<p><A HREF="saltwater.html"><IMG SRC="images/kingfish.jpg"
WIDTH="192" HEIGHT="128" ALT="Picture of a man holding up a large
Kingfish" border="0" align="right"></A>

<P>The oceans offer an endless variety of game species, from
inshore favorites to offshore tackle-busters. This nice Kingfish
was caught on a Sardine minnow slow-trolled off the beach. The
Saltwater section of our guide contains all the information you
need to pursue the ocean's most pleasant piscatorial prizes.
Permit and Pompano await you!

    <H2>Freshwater Fishing</H2>

<P><A HREF="freshwater.html"><IMG SRC="images/pargo.jpg"
WIDTH="192" HEIGHT="128" ALT="Picture of a man holding up a Pargo"
BORDER="0" ALIGN="left"></A>

<P>Some of the most avidly pursued fish swim in fresh water, from
the majestic trout and salmon of northern waters to the wily
largemouth bass. Whether you fish on an idyllic stream with dry
flies, or zip around in your Bass boat on the lazy reservoirs and
rivers of the Old South, our Fishing Guide has the stuff you need.
```

Note that we have moved both IMG tags to place them before their accompanying text. When using the ALIGN attribute, an IMG tag must come before the text that is to wrap around it. Also notice that we've made the text longer to demonstrate the text-wrap effect. Figure 8-5 shows the result.

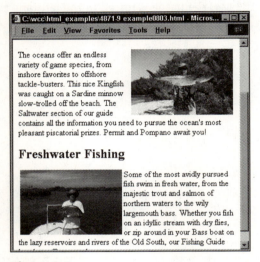

Figure 8-5
The ALIGN attribute enables you to wrap text around an image. The top IMG tag includes ALIGN="right"; the bottom image is set to ALIGN="left."

The only problem with this page is that the text is too close to the image. To create a bit of white space between image and text, use the optional Horizontal Space (HSPACE) and Vertical Space (VSPACE) attributes, as in Listing 8-4:

Listing 8-4:

```
<IMG SRC="images/kingfish.jpg" WIDTH="192" HEIGHT="128"
ALT="Picture of a man holding up a large Kingfish" BORDER="0"
ALIGN="left" HSPACE="8" VSPACE="16">
```

This creates a margin of 8 pixels on the horizontal edge of the image and a margin of 16 pixels on the vertical edge. Usually, I find that it works best when VSPACE has a larger value than HSPACE, but experiment with other values to find what looks best on your pages. Naturally, this is one of those things that should be consistent throughout a particular Web site.

Figure 8-6 shows what the page looks like with the HSPACE and VSPACE values shown in Listing 8-4.

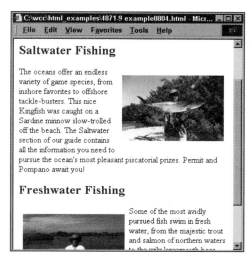

Figure 8-6
Use the ALIGN, HSPACE, and VSPACE attributes to create attractive text-wrapping effects as shown here.

Done!

REVIEW

In this session, you have learned several techniques for integrating an image into a Web page. This has included:

- Making an image a hyperlink
- Specifying an image as a page background
- Wrapping text around an image

QUIZ YOURSELF

1. Hyperlinked images have a border by default. What must you do if you don't want the image to have a border? (See "Making an Image a Hyperlink.")
2. What is the purpose of a teaser or thumbnail image? (See "Creating Thumbnail Images.")

3. Which tag can specify a background image for a page? (See "Defining a Background Image.")

4. Which tag is used to wrap text around a graphic image? (See "Wrapping Text Around Graphics.")

5. Which attributes are used to create a margin between an image and wrapped text? (See "Wrapping Text Around Graphics.")

Creating Quality Graphics

Session Checklist

✔ Understanding various graphic file formats

✔ Minimizing graphic load times

✔ Creating a logo by using graphic text

You've learned to add existing graphics to Web pages in several ways. Now you learn to create and modify your own graphics using your choice of graphic-editing software.

**30 Min.
To Go**

Using Graphic-Editing Software

There are many graphic-editing software packages available, covering all price ranges, and just about any of them can be used to create quality graphics for the Web. The examples in this book use Jasc Paint Shop Pro, which is on this book's CD-ROM companion. The rudimentary Microsoft Paint is included in most versions of Windows (choose Start ➪ Programs ➪ Accessories ➪ Paint). Lview Pro (http://www.lview.com/) is a feature-rich shareware product for Windows. Pricier options include Adobe Photoshop (Windows and Mac. See http://www.adobe.com) and Corel's suite of products (Windows, Mac and Linux. See http://www.corel.com).

The basic features and functions of all graphic editors are pretty similar, so you should have no trouble applying the techniques discussed here to any software package you may choose to use.

Types of graphic formats

Traditionally, graphic editors fall into two categories: *vector-based* and *bitmap-based*. The vector-based editors are often called Draw programs, and the bitmap-based (or *raster-based*) editors are often called Paint programs. CorelDRAW and Adobe Illustrator are vector-based graphic editors, and Microsoft Paint, Corel PHOTO-PAINT and Adobe Photoshop are bitmap-based graphic editors. Actually, some of the latest products, including Jasc Paint Shop Pro, include elements of both approaches.

As you may already know, computer graphics work by dividing an image into tiny squares called pixels, each of which is assigned a particular color. A bitmap-based graphic editor stores the value for each pixel (and usually allows you to edit each pixel individually if desired). Using a bitmap-based editor, any graphic image of a given size contains a fixed number of numeric values (one for each pixel), regardless of what the image is.

A vector-based graphic file, however, stores a set of instructions for creating an image rather than storing a value for each pixel. Therefore, vector graphic files are much smaller, and often can be edited in more flexible ways, than bitmap graphic files. The vector-based format is ideal for things such as line art and text/graphic combinations, whereas the bitmap-based format is necessary for photographs.

Although most graphic editors have their own proprietary file formats, there are several standard formats for bitmap-based graphics, including .tif and .bmp. Most modern editing software can open and save files in a wide variety of formats. Graphics for the Web, however, must be in one of three formats: .gif, .jpg, or the newer and rare .png. GIF (*graphics interchange format,* pronounced "giff" or "jiff") and JPG (pronounced "jay-peg") are compressed file formats designed to load quickly over the Internet.

Keeping load time low

**20 Min.
To Go**

As you have learned in Session 8, graphic files are much larger than text files and can cause unacceptably long load times unless steps are taken to keep them small. Today's computers are capable of displaying full-screen images of extremely high quality, but the Internet is not capable of transferring such images at an acceptable speed. Therefore, the name of the game is to reduce graphic file size without sacrificing too much quality.

There are several policies that can help keep page-load times down, all of which you should follow. Two of them are built into the Web, so to speak:

- *Compressed file formats*. The `.gif` and `.jpg` formats both use a form of file compression to reduce file sizes. They are both *lossy* compression schemes, which means that the original image can't be recreated from the compressed form, as a certain amount of data has been discarded from the file. `.gif` and `.jpg` are not high-quality formats for acquiring and editing source files but are designed to be end-user formats for delivery over the Web.

- *Low resolution*. The *resolution* of a graphic image refers to the number of pixels used to represent it. The higher the resolution, the higher the image quality, and the larger the file size. Web browsers display images at a resolution of 72 pixels per inch. By way of comparison, most home printers print at 300 or 600 dots per inch; professional printing often happens at 1200 or even 2400 dots per inch.

By now, you probably perceive that the main consideration with Web graphics isn't to achieve the highest image quality but to deliver a fairly high level of quality while keeping download times short. You can do several things to reduce load times without sacrificing quality:

- *Keep images small*. Smaller physical images translate to smaller file sizes, so most Web sites favor small images, three or four inches wide at the most. Several small images usually load faster than one big one and can often tell your story more effectively. Get the most out of your images by cropping them tightly and keeping them simple.

- *Use images sparingly*. Use images only where they are necessary to get your point across. Think carefully before replacing text headings or logos with graphic files.

- *Use IMG attributes*. In Session 7, you learn to use the ALT, HEIGHT, and WIDTH attributes of the IMG tag. Although these attributes don't affect the load time of an image, they help a lot in reducing the problems of slow page loads. Always use them.

Building a Logo

Enough theory for now. Let's open our graphic editor and start creating some original graphics. Freddy's Fishing Guide needs a logo to make the pages more attractive and to reinforce a consistent brand throughout the site.

Consistency is one of the marks of quality graphics. Once you've created a logo, it should be used throughout your site. If you're creating a Web site for an existing company or putting content from another medium online, any logos and other graphic elements on your site should match existing graphic elements used in print or other media.

In this example, you create a logo by using Paint Shop Pro. If you are using some other software, the exact commands differ, but the basic process is the same.

1. Open Paint Shop Pro, and select File ⇨ New to start a new file.

2. The New Image dialog box appears, as shown in Figure 9-1. Set Width to 468 pixels, Height to 60 pixels, and Resolution to 72 pixels/inch (the exact size doesn't matter, but we've chosen 468×60 because it's a standard size for Web banners). Set Background color to White and Image type to 256 Colors (8 Bit).

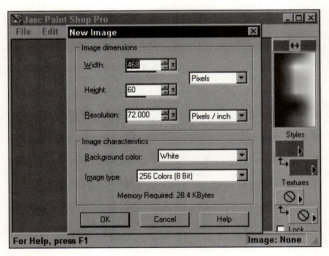

Figure 9-1
Setting parameters for a new Web-graphic file in Paint Shop Pro

3. Choose the Text tool (represented by a capital A), and click on the image to bring up the Text Entry dialog box, as shown in Figure 9-2.

4. Select a font (Comic Sans MS in our example), and set the type size to 20 points. Select both Bold and Italic.

5. In the Styles section on the left, click Fill color, and select a dark blue.

6. Type the name of your Web site into the Text box.

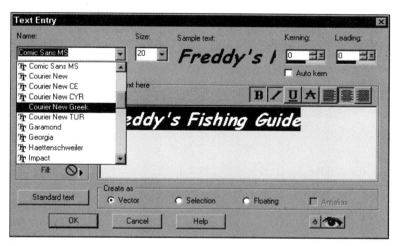

Figure 9-2
The Text Entry dialog box gives you many options for controlling the appearance of text.

7. Select OK. The text should appear in the image, with the color, size, and styles you have specified in the Text Entry dialog box.

8. The text appears with handles that can be used to move or resize it. Drag it by the center handle until it is centered. Size it using a corner handle so that it takes up most of the canvas. To size an element while preserving its proportions, use the right mouse button to click the sizing handle. Figure 9-3 shows the resulting logo.

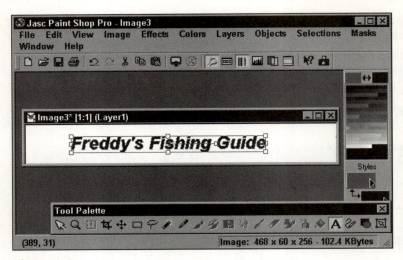

Figure 9-3
Square handles are used to move or resize an image.

9. Choose File ⇨ Save As. In the Save As dialog box, choose the file type "CompuServe Graphics Interchange (.gif)." This is the official name for the file format, but most people just say "GIF." Give it a descriptive name such as "freds_logo.gif".

10. Open index.html in your Web editor. In Session 2 we created a text heading by using the H1 tag (Listing 2-2). Replace this heading with the graphic heading we have just created, by modifying the code as follows (Listing 9-1):

Listing 9-1:

```
<H3><A HREF="http://www.hungryminds.com/">Hungry Minds
Presents</A>:</H3>


<IMG SRC="images/freds_logo.gif" HEIGHT="60" WIDTH="468"
ALT="Freddy's Fishing Guide Logo">


<H2>
<A HREF="saltwater.html">Saltwater Fishing</A>
</H2>
```

Figure 9-4 shows the resulting page. Instead of an HTML text heading, Freddy's home page now has a graphic heading. Using graphic text such as this has the advantage that you can use any font and style you like and create much more elaborate text than you can by using HTML text. The disadvantages are increased page-load time and the fact that graphic text is more difficult to modify later.

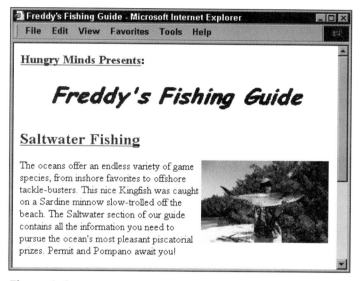

Figure 9-4
The main heading for Freddy's home page is now a graphic element. Using graphic elements instead of HTML text for logos and headings enables you to give your Web pages a more distinctive appearance.

REVIEW

Done!

In this session, you have learned to create a graphic to use in a Web page. This has included:

- Understanding the characteristics of various graphic file formats
- Learning ways to minimize load time
- Creating a graphic text element to use as a heading

QUIZ YOURSELF

1. What are the two main types of graphic editors? (See "Types of Graphic Formats.")

2. What are the three graphic formats used for Web graphics? (See "Types of Graphic Formats.")

3. Which pixel resolution is used for Web graphics? (See "Keeping Load Time Low.")

4. What is the main goal to keep in mind when creating graphics for the Web? (See "Keeping Load Time Low.")

5. What are the pros and cons of using a graphic image as opposed to plain HTML text? (See "Building a Logo.")

SESSION

10

Optimizing Graphics for the Web

Session Checklist

✔ Choosing the .jpg or .gif format

✔ Understanding transparent and interlaced images

✔ Using Web-safe colors

**30 Min.
To Go**

You've probably noticed that we choose the .gif format for the logo we create in Session 9, although the photos we add in Session 7 are in the .jpg format. This is because the way in which the .jpg format compresses an image works better for photographs, whereas .gif compression works better for other types of images such as artwork and graphic text.

Choosing the Best Format: .jpg or .gif?

You don't need to know the technical reasons behind it; just remember this: always use .jpg for photos and .gif for everything else (the newer .png format is similar to .gif). The distinction is a fairly subtle one, and you can get perfectly acceptable results using .gif for photos and vice versa. The world won't end just because you use the .jpg format for line art or the .gif format for a photo, but you'll get slightly better quality with smaller file sizes if you follow the standard procedure: .jpgs for photos and .gifs for all other graphics.

The `.gif` format has a couple of special features that are handy for Web use: `.gif` images can be made transparent and/or interlaced.

Creating transparent images

In a transparent `.gif` image, one color (normally the background color) can be transparent. When the image is placed on a Web page, the background color of the page shows through the transparent part. Figure 10-1 shows a transparent and a non-transparent `.gif` on a Web page with a light blue background.

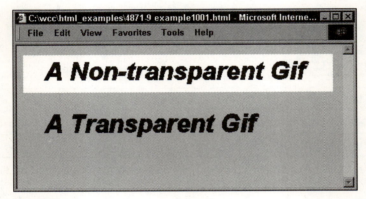

Figure 10-1
The upper image is a non-transparent .gif; the lower image is transparent. The non-transparent image appears as a rectangle with its white background color.

Of course, if the background color of the image is the same as the background color of the Web page, there is no visible difference between a transparent and a non-transparent image. This is the case in Session 9, as the Freddy's Fishing Guide logo has a white background.

Setting a background color for a page

But wait! Haven't we jumped the gun a bit? After all, we haven't yet learned to set a background color for a Web page. In fact, it's very easy. You can do so by using the BGCOLOR attribute of the BODY tag, as in this example:

```
<BODY BGCOLOR="black">
```

You have learned to specify colors in Session 6. The most common colors can be referenced by their names, but others must be specified by a string of three two-digit hexadecimal numbers.

Conflect p 76
FFFFFF ?

```
<BODY BGCOLOR="#000000">
```

This code example produces the same result as the previous one, as 000000 is the numerical equivalent of black.

When saving a `.gif` file, you must specify whether it is to be transparent, and you can choose a particular color to make transparent (this should be the background color of the image). In Paint Shop Pro, this is done by selecting Save As ➪ Options ➪ Run Optimizer.

When should you use a transparent `.gif`? Use it for anything that you want to float above the page, without a rectangular background. Usually, logos and other graphic text are transparent. Photos should not be transparent (and should be in the `.jpg` format anyway, which doesn't allow transparency). Transparent `.gifs` are probably more common than non-transparent ones, which is why many graphic editors create them by default.

An ad banner is one type of graphic that should *never* be transparent. Generally, an ad banner is intended to be displayed on various sites, and you have no way of knowing which background color any of those sites may be using. If the banner is transparent, the page background color appears as the background color of the banner, creating a very different effect than the designer has intended.

Using interlaced .gifs

**20 Min.
To Go**

Another handy feature of the `.gif` format is called *interlacing*. An ordinary `.gif` loads from top to bottom, one line of pixels at a time. If the file is large and/or the user's Internet connection is slow, this can be a trial of patience, as the user can't tell what the image is supposed to be until it is fully loaded. An interlaced `.gif`, however, loads in sets of alternate lines so that it first appears as a blurry image, which gradually solidifies into its final form.

Although an interlaced `.gif` does not load faster (in fact, it loads a bit more slowly), it makes the Web page seem to load a bit faster, as the viewer can get an idea of what each image looks like before it is fully loaded (and perhaps decide whether it's worth waiting for the whole page to load). Like transparency, interlacing is an option that can be chosen when you save a `.gif` file. In Paint Shop Pro, select Save As ➪ Options.

Preserving image quality

As you learn in Session 7, Web graphics are delivered in compressed file formats at a low resolution, in order to keep file sizes small. This doesn't mean that Web images must be of low quality. Terrible-looking graphics are common on Web sites, but this is only because site designers haven't taken care to prepare them correctly. To ensure that your images are of the highest quality possible, follow these rules:

1. Never edit a .gif, .jpg or .png file directly. These compressed formats are intended to be used only for the final presentation of an image. Although you can open and edit these files, doing so sometimes causes them to become distorted. Do all your editing in your graphic editor's native file format. If you think you might make changes to an image later, be sure to save a version of the image in the native format, and use this version for any future edits. If you need to open a file in a different graphic editor than the one you used to create it, save it in a high-quality format such as .bmp or .tif.

2. When converting an image to digital form (using a scanner or digital camera), always do so at a high quality level. Many people mistakenly believe that because the end product will be delivered at 72 dpi, there's no reason to use a higher resolution when acquiring and editing an image. This isn't true: set your digital camera or scanner to a high resolution such as 600 dpi, and convert to 72 dpi only in the very last step of editing.

3. Slight differences in the algorithms that a graphic editor uses to convert an image to a .gif file can make big differences in file size. *Optimizing* a .gif file can often reduce the file size with no reduction in quality. Advanced graphic editors such as Adobe Photoshop have built-in optimizing capabilities. If you choose the "Save for Web" option in Photoshop, it shows you several possible end-result files and lets you choose the best one. Several stand-alone image optimizing software products are available, including GIF Wizard (http://www.gifwizard.com/) and Ulead SmartSaver Pro (http://www.ulead.com/).

10 Min. To Go

About Web-safe Colors

In Session 6, you learn to specify a color (for a background, text, or other element) by using a string of three two-digit hexadecimal numbers. This gives you a lot of options: over 16 million, in fact. For you technically inclined folks, this is 24-bit color.

However, not all users' systems are capable of displaying 24-bit color. Older monitors and/or legacy-browser versions may only be capable of 8-bit color. To further complicate things, Windows and Mac systems may display the same color slightly differently. If a browser can't display the exact color specified, it automatically chooses whatever it deems to be the closest match available. In some cases, the results may be far from what the designer has intended. (In Session 6, you encounter a similar situation in regard to fonts.)

You can ensure that your colors look the same on all users' systems by using the *Web-safe (or browser-safe) color palette*. A *palette* (also called a *color look-up table*) is the set of colors available to a particular application. The Web-safe palette consists of 216 colors, which should be displayed consistently on any system capable of at least 8-bit color (256 colors).

How do you know if a particular color is Web-safe? Every color is represented in HTML by three pairs of digits. For all colors in the Web-safe palette, each of these pairs must have one of the following values:

```
00, 33, 66, 99, CC, FF
```

Examples of Web-safe colors include:

```
000000 (black)
003366
006699
66CC99
CCCCFF
FFFFFF (white)
```

page 76 says the opposite

The 6×6×6 Browser-safe Color Cube, which you can find on the Web at `http://wdvl.com/Authoring/Graphics/Colour/666.html`, is a very handy tool that shows all the Web-safe colors with their numeric equivalents. Any time you need to specify a color in HTML code, you can pop over there, select the perfect color, and simply copy and paste the value.

When creating graphics by using a graphic editor, you don't need to worry about all this as long as you make sure the editor has the Web-safe palette loaded. Most editing software lets you load different palettes for various applications. In Paint Shop Pro, choose Colors ⇨ Load Palette, then load `Safety.pal`. Once this palette is loaded, anything you create uses only the Web-safe colors. To see the HTML equivalent of any color, simply click one of the little color squares at the top right of the screen. This brings up the Select Color From Palette dialog box, in which the HTML value of the selected color shows up at the bottom right, as shown in Figure 10-2.

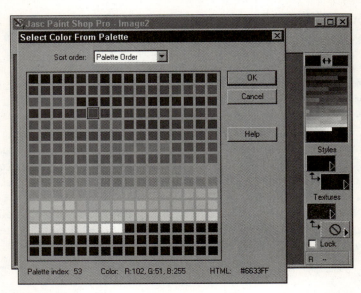

Figure 10-2
Selecting a color from the 216-color Web-safe palette in Paint Shop Pro. Note
the bottom of the dialog box, where both the RGB value and the HTML
(hexadecimal) value for the selected color are shown.

Done!

REVIEW

In this session, you have learned some ways to optimize the quality of your Web graphics. This has included:

- Choosing an appropriate file format
- Using transparent and interlaced `.gif`s
- Understanding Web-safe colors

QUIZ YOURSELF

1. Which Web-graphic format is best to use for photographs? (See "Choosing the Best Format: `.jpg` or `.gif`?")

2. Name one situation in which a transparent image should definitely not be used. (See " Setting a Background Color for a Page.")

3. Does an interlaced .gif load faster than a non-interlaced .gif? (See "Using Interlaced .gifs.")

4. What is the purpose of using the Web-safe color palette? (See "About Web-safe Colors.")

5. Which of these three values represents a Web-safe color: CC3300; 67CCFF, AACC00 (See "About Web-safe Colors.")

PART

II

Saturday Morning

1. What tag can you use to create bold text? Italic text?
2. Why is using underlined text as a means of emphasis not recommended?
3. What two tags do you use to create an ordered list?
4. Define an attribute, and give an example.
5. What happens if a FONT tag specifies a typeface that isn't available on the user's system?
6. Is it best to set body text in a serif or sans-serif font?
7. How can you specify the color black within a FONT tag?
8. What numeric system does HTML use to specify color values?
9. What is the effect of including this attribute in a FONT tag: SIZE="-2"?
10. Should you use an absolute or a relative address when linking to a file within the same site?
11. What's the purpose of using the WIDTH and HEIGHT attributes?
12. What are three reasons to use the ALT attribute of the IMG tag?
13. What code do you use to create an IMG tag with no border?
14. What must you do to create a hyperlinked image with no border?
15. How do you wrap text around a graphic image?
16. How can you create a margin between an image and wrapped text?
17. What are the three graphic formats used for Web graphics?

18. Which graphic format is best for photographs?

19. What is the Web-safe color palette?

20. Of these three values, which represents a Web-safe color? CC3300, 69BBFF, AACC11

PART

III

Saturday Afternoon

SESSION

11

Using Tables

Session Checklist

✔ Creating a basic table

✔ Sizing a table

✔ Specifying background colors, alignment, and other table
  attributes

**30 Min.
To Go**

Y ou've learned to create various types of text elements, to include graphics in your pages, and to combine the two elegantly. Thus far, you've arranged elements in a sequential way (that is, each element follows the preceding one vertically down the page). In this session, you learn to use HTML tables, which enable you to arrange elements in rows and columns.

Table Basics: TABLE, TR, and TD tags

You can build a table by using three tags: TABLE, Table Row (TR), and Table Data (TD). A table is made up of one or more Table Rows, and each Table Row is made up of one or more Table Data elements. Listing 11-1 shows a simple table of two rows and two columns:

Listing 11-1:

```
<TABLE BORDER="2">
  <TR>
      <TD>
      Item 1
      </TD>
      <TD>
      Item 2
      </TD>
  </TR>

  <TR>
      <TD>
      Item 3
      </TD>
      <TD>
      Item 4
      </TD>
  </TR>

</TABLE>
```

The resulting Web page can be seen in Figure 11-1.

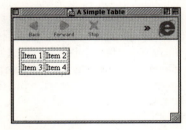

Figure 11-1
A simple table of two rows and two columns. Note the border, which we create by including BORDER="2" in the TABLE element.

Note these facts about tables:

- TABLE, TR, and TD must be used in strict hierarchy and must be nested correctly. In other words, TD tags are contained within TR tags, and TR tags are contained within TABLE tags.

- Always use closing tags. Although in some cases a table may be displayed as desired even if some closing tags are omitted, in other cases this may cause big problems; get in the habit of using all Table-related tags in pairs.

- Every Row (TR) in a table must have the same number of cells (TD) unless you are using COLSPAN or ROWSPAN, as explained later in this session.

- In Session 2, you learn to use indents and line breaks to make your HTML code easier to read and to edit. When coding tables, it's customary to indent each nested set of tags one level (that is, indent TR tags one level and TD tags two levels). Tables can get very complex, so follow good coding habits to save yourself editing time later.

The space contained within a pair of TD tags is called a *table cell*. Table cells can contain text, images, hyperlinks or any other element, including other tables.

**20 Min.
To Go**

Sizing Tables

Entire tables, or individual table cells, can be sized by using the optional WIDTH attribute. Values for WIDTH can be expressed *relatively* (as a percentage of page width) or *absolutely* (in pixels). Listing 11-2 contains two tables. The first table has WIDTH defined as 50 percent, so it covers half the width of the browser window. The second table has WIDTH defined as 100 percent, so it covers the entire width of the window. In both tables, we've set the width of the first table cell in each row at 40 percent and the width of the second table cell at 60 percent, so the second column is wider than the first. Figure 11-2 shows the resulting page.

Listing 11-2:

```
<TABLE WIDTH="50%" BORDER="2">

   <TR>
      <TD WIDTH="40%">
      Tarpon
      </TD>
      <TD WIDTH="60%">
      <IMG SRC="images/tarpon_small.jpg" WIDTH="100" HEIGHT="31"
BORDER="0" ALT="Picture of a Tarpon">
      </TD>
   </TR>
```

Continued

Part III—Saturday Afternoon
Session 11

Listing 11-2 *(continued)*

```
   <TR>
      <TD WIDTH="40%">
      Pargo
      </TD>
      <TD WIDTH="60%">
      <IMG SRC="images/pargo_small.jpg" WIDTH="100" HEIGHT="31"
BORDER="0" ALT="Picture of a Pargo">
      </TD>
   </TR>

</TABLE>

<TABLE WIDTH="100%" BORDER="2">

   <TR>
      <TD WIDTH="40%">
      Tarpon
      </TD>
      <TD WIDTH="60%">
      <IMG SRC="images/tarpon_small.jpg" WIDTH="100" HEIGHT="31"
BORDER="0" ALT="Picture of a Tarpon">
      </TD>
   </TR>

   <TR>
      <TD WIDTH="40%">
      Pargo
      </TD>
      <TD WIDTH="60%">
      <IMG SRC="images/pargo_small.jpg" WIDTH="100" HEIGHT="31"
BORDER="0" ALT="Picture of a Pargo">
      </TD>
   </TR>

</TABLE>
```

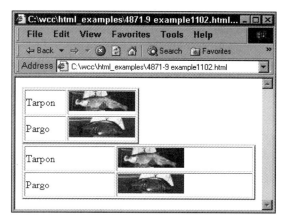

Figure 11-2
The width of both these tables is relative to the width of the browser window. The top table is half the width of the window, and the lower table covers the full width of the window.

To get an idea of how relative widths work, go through the following steps (this may not work with some old legacy browsers):

1. Launch your Web browser, and open Listing 11-2 (`html_examples/ example1102.html` on the CD-ROM).

2. Click the Restore button at the upper right of the browser window so that the window is not full screen.

3. Grab a corner of the window with your mouse, and move the mouse so that the size of the window changes. You should see the size of the tables change with it.

4. If you make the window smaller, the tables get smaller too, but they cannot get any smaller than the largest element contained in one of the table cells. This is an important point to remember: no matter what size you specify for a table cell, it stretches to accommodate any image or other fixed-size element you place within it.

The TABLE tags in Listing 11-2 specified relative widths. Now try setting an absolute size in pixels by changing the TABLE tags as follows:

```
<TABLE WIDTH="400" BORDER="2">
```

for the first table, and:

```
<TABLE WIDTH="600" BORDER="2">
```

for the second table.

Open the revised file (Listing 11-3 on the CD-ROM) in your browser, and repeat the preceding steps. This time the size of the tables does not change as you change the window size. Figure 11-3 shows the result, with part of the table running off the screen.

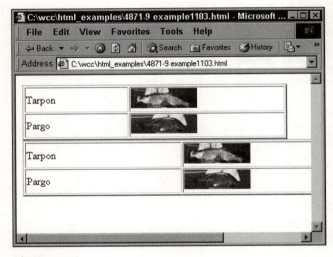

Figure 11-3
These tables have been assigned an absolute size, so they do not expand or contract to fit the browser window. Note the scroll bar at the bottom of the window.

If a table (or any other element) is too wide for a user's browser window, a scroll bar appears at the bottom of the window, and the user needs to scroll to the right to see the rest of the table. Good designers try to avoid scrolling when practical, so you may want to think twice before setting an absolute size for table elements.

Other Useful Table Attributes

Tables are very versatile. By using some of the optional attributes, and a little imagination, you can get many useful effects.

**10 Min.
To Go**

Using the BGCOLOR attribute

TABLE, TR, and TD tags can all take the optional BGCOLOR attribute, which sets a background color. In Listing 11-4, we've set a light blue color as the background for the entire table and a darker blue as the background for the first cell (shown in Figure 11-4):

Listing 11-4:

```
<TABLE WIDTH="50%" BORDER="2" BGCOLOR="#00FFFF">

    <TR>
        <TD WIDTH="40%" BGCOLOR="#0000FF">
        Tarpon
        </TD>
        <TD WIDTH="60%">
        <IMG SRC="images/tarpon_small.jpg" WIDTH="100" HEIGHT="31"
BORDER="0" ALT="Picture of a Tarpon">
        </TD>
    </TR>

    <TR>
        <TD WIDTH="40%">
        Pargo
        </TD>
        <TD WIDTH="60%">
        <IMG SRC="images/pargo_small.jpg" WIDTH="100" HEIGHT="31"
BORDER="0" ALT="Picture of a Pargo">
        </TD>
    </TR>

</TABLE>
```

Note a few things:

- BGCOLOR set in the TD tag overrides BGCOLOR set in the TABLE tag.
- Colors are specified using the same six-digit code you learn in Session 6.
- Background colors in tables, as well as some of the other optional attributes, don't work in some older legacy browsers.

Figure 11-4
The darker background color of the first table cell overrides the lighter color that has been set as a background for the entire table.

Using ALIGN and VALIGN attributes

You can control how the contents of a table cell line up by using the ALIGN (horizontal alignment) and VALIGN (vertical alignment) attributes. Possible values for ALIGN include left, right, and center. Possible values for VALIGN include top, bottom, and middle. For example, to center an image in a table cell, use the following code:

```
<TD ALIGN="center" VALIGN="middle">
<IMG SRC="image.jpg">
</TD>
```

Using COLSPAN and ROWSPAN attributes

You can make a table cell span several columns by using the COLSPAN attribute of the TD tag. This is useful for creating a heading that stretches across all the columns of a table. Similarly, ROWSPAN creates a cell that stretches vertically across the rows of a table. For example, the following code creates a wide table cell stretching across three columns:

```
<TD COLSPAN="3">
A Heading for Your Table
</TD>
```

When using `COLSPAN`, **don't use** `WIDTH`; **the width of the cell is determined by the width of the cells it spans. Also note that the cell in this example counts as three cells (because of** `COLSPAN="3"`**), so it is the only cell in its row.**

In Listing 11-5, we've created a fairly complex table of four rows and three columns by using the `BGCOLOR`, `COLSPAN`, `ALIGN`, and `VALIGN` attributes. Figure 11-5 shows how the table appears in a browser.

Listing 11-5:

```
<TABLE WIDTH="100%" BORDER="2">

   <TR>
      <TD COLSPAN="3" ALIGN="center" VALIGN="middle"
BGCOLOR="#00FFFF">
      <A HREF="saltwater.html"><STRONG>Saltwater Fish</STRONG></A>
      </TD>
   </TR>

   <TR>
      <TD ALIGN="center" VALIGN="middle">
      <STRONG>Name</STRONG>
      </TD>
      <TD ALIGN="center" VALIGN="middle">
      <STRONG>Photo</STRONG>
      </TD>
      <TD ALIGN="center" VALIGN="middle">
      <STRONG>Favorite Bait</STRONG>
      </TD>
   </TR>

   <TR>
      <TD>
      Pargo
      </TD>
      <TD ALIGN="center" VALIGN="middle">
      <IMG SRC="images/pargo_small.jpg" WIDTH="100" HEIGHT="31"
BORDER="0" ALT="Picture of a Pargo">
      </TD>
      <TD>
```

Continued

Listing 11-5 *(continued)*

```
        Live Fish or Shrimp
        </TD>
    </TR>

    <TR>
        <TD>
        Tarpon
        </TD>
        <TD ALIGN="center" VALIGN="middle">
        <IMG SRC="images/tarpon_small.jpg" WIDTH="100" HEIGHT="31"
BORDER="0" ALT="Picture of a Tarpon">
        </TD>
        <TD>
        Large Fish
        </TD>
    </TR>

</TABLE>
```

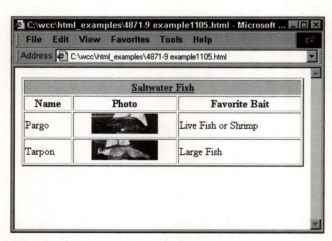

Figure 11-5
This table uses COLSPAN to create a heading, as well as alignment attributes to center some of the elements in the cells.

Tables are an important page-layout tool, as you learn in Session 12. They can and do get much more complex, so be sure you understand the material in this session before moving on.

Done!

REVIEW

In this session, you have learned to arrange elements in rows and columns by using tables. This has included:

- Using TABLE, TR, and TD Tags
- Specifying a size for a table or for an individual table cell
- Using optional attributes to customize your tables further

QUIZ YOURSELF

1. What is the relationship among the TABLE, TR, and TD tags? (See "Table Basics: TABLE, TR, TD Tags.")

2. What attribute is used to set the width of a table or a table cell? (See "Sizing Tables.")

3. In what two ways can the width of a table or cell be expressed? (See "Sizing Tables.")

4. How do you center an element within a table cell? (See "Using ALIGN and VALIGN Attributes.")

5. What attribute is used to create a horizontal heading spanning several table cells? (See "Using COLSPAN and ROWSPAN Attributes.")

Advanced Formatting with Tables

Session Checklist

✔ Using tables without borders for page-layout purposes

✔ Arranging text in newspaper-style columns

✔ Creating a sidebar

30 Min. To Go

I n Session 11, you learn to use tables to present information in rows and columns. This tabular format is quite useful and is seen often in Web pages. However, HTML tables are not limited to traditional table applications of this kind. In this session, you learn to use tables without borders as a powerful page-layout tool. You can use tables to create newspaper-style columns, and to arrange text in sidebars, top bars or bottom bars.

Getting Away from the Linear Look

You can transform a table from a tool for presenting tabular data into a tool for positioning elements on a Web page simply by getting rid of the border. Open the

HTML file you have created in Listing 11-4; remove the BGCOLOR attribute, and change the BORDER attribute of the TABLE tag to zero:

```
<TABLE WIDTH="50%" BORDER="0">
```

Figure 12-1 shows the resulting page.

Figure 12-1
The table itself is now invisible because the BORDER attribute has been set to zero (BORDER="0"). Only the content elements (text and graphics) are visible, but the table determines their position on the page.

Tables weren't intended to be used in this way, and HTML purists don't approve of using tables to position elements on a page. However, until Cascading Style Sheets (CSS) were introduced, tables were the only tool available, and many existing sites use them extensively. In Session 19, you learn the more modern, and more powerful, technique of using style sheets for positioning. Like using the FONT tag, however, using tables for positioning is something you should understand because so many sites use the technique and because some of the positioning concepts you learn along the way will be useful later.

Arranging text in columns

The side-by-side columns used by newspapers and magazines serve an important purpose. The eye has difficulty following text if the lines are too long. Dividing a page of text into vertical columns makes it much easier to read. In addition, columns enable you to present more information on a single page, as you can present several articles or other groups of text side by side.

Create a newspaper-style format, with a heading and two columns, with the following HTML code (Listing 12-1):

Listing 12-1:

```
<TABLE WIDTH="100%" BORDER="0">
<TR>
<TD COLSPAN="2">
<H1>Bass Fishing In Tennessee</H1>
</TD>
</TR>
<TR>
<TD WIDTH="50%">
Insert lengthy example text here.
The lakes, reservoirs and rivers of Tennessee are chock-full of
Bass, and thousands of anglers descend upon the poor innocents
daily. Some use live bait, but true Bassers stick with artificial
lures, shunning live bait as unsportsmanlike.
<P>The plastic worm is favored for fishing brushpiles, while the
"jig and pig" is often used for fishing rocky dropoffs.
</TD>
<TD WIDTH="50%">
Insert second half of example text here.
</TD>
</TR>
</TABLE>
```

Figure 12-2 shows the resulting page in Internet Explorer, and Figure 12-3 shows exactly the same page in the Netscape browser.

Part III—Saturday Afternoon
Session 12

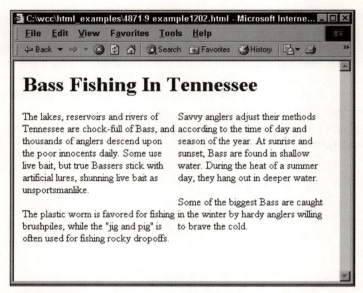

Figure 12-2
This is a common way to format a unit of text, with a heading spanning two columns (COLSPAN="2") of body text. Here we see the example page displayed in Internet Explorer.

Limitations of the columnar approach

The layout we've just created is a very common one in print, but it's less common on the Web for two reasons:

1. *Text doesn't flow between columns*. When a print publisher lays out text in a columnar format such as this, each column is assigned a certain length, and the text is broken wherever it needs to break to make the columns of equal length. With a word processor such as Word or a DTP program such as Quark or Pagemaker, this is easy to do, as text flows automatically from one column to the next. Simply adjust the column length to produce a neat, symmetrical layout. Unfortunately, HTML tables offer no way to do this, so you must choose a point at which to split the text into two sections, placing each section in its own table cell. It's difficult to choose the perfect spot to break the text, and a bit of blank space at the end of the second column is the usual result.

2. *Browsers display text slightly differently*. Compare Figure 12-2 with Figure 12-3, and you see that the end of the second column does not occur in exactly the same place. This effect is even more pronounced with older browser versions. A two-column layout that lines up perfectly in one browser may have a few lines of white space at the end in another browser.

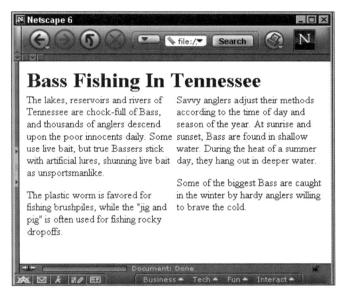

Figure 12-3
This figure shows exactly the same file as Figure 12-2, but this time we are viewing it in the Netscape browser. Note the very slight difference in the way the text lines up.

Creating a Sidebar

**20 Min.
To Go**

Another way of arranging elements on a page, common in print magazines and extremely common in Web pages, is a *sidebar*. A sidebar is a vertical division of a page used to present information that is separate from the main text. A sidebar can contain definitions, cross-references, or other things that refer to the main text (or perhaps simply a bit of information related to, but separate from, the main text). In Web pages, sidebars are used often to present navigational elements, which link to the main sections of a Web site, and to present ads.

Part III—Saturday Afternoon
Session 12

Create a typical Web page that has a left sidebar by using the following code (Listing 12-2):

Listing 12-2:

```
<TABLE WIDTH="100%" BORDER="0">
<TR>
<TD COLSPAN="2">
<H1>Saltwater Fishing</H2>
<TD>
</TR>
<TR>
<TD WIDTH="30%" BGCOLOR="#00FFFF" VALIGN="left">
<P><A HREF="index.html"><STRONG>Home</STRONG></A>
<P><A HREF="saltwater.html"><STRONG>Saltwater</STRONG></A>
<P><A HREF="freshwater.html"><STRONG>Freshwater</STRONG></A>
</TD>
<TD WIDTH="70%">
<IMG SRC="images/kingfish.jpg" WIDTH="192" HEIGHT="128"
ALT="Picture of a man holding up a large Kingfish" BORDER="0"
ALIGN="left" HSPACE="8" VSPACE="16">
<P>The oceans offer an endless variety of game species, from
inshore favorites to offshore tackle-busters. This nice Kingfish
was caught on a Sardine minnow slow-trolled off the beach. The
Saltwater section of our guide contains all the information you
need to pursue the ocean's most pleasant piscatorial prizes.
Permit and Pompano await you!
</TD>
</TR>
</TABLE>
```

The resulting Web page is shown in Figure 12-4. We've created a left sidebar that is 30 percent of the width of the page. Of course, a page can have either a left or a right sidebar, or even both, and any desired width can be specified in either percentage or pixel values. It's common to make a sidebar stand out a little by giving it a contrasting background color, as in Figure 12-4.

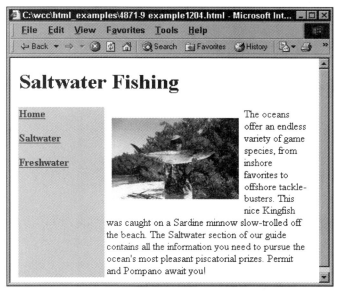

Figure 12-4
A typical left-hand sidebar. To get a feel for how this sort of page-layout technique enables you to present more information on a page, compare this page with the more linear ones we've created in previous sessions.

**10 Min.
To Go**

Using the CELLPADDING attribute

There's only one problem with the page you've just created. The text doesn't look quite right because it's too close to the edges of the sidebar. Both the left-hand sidebar and the right-hand body text would look much better with a small margin. You can easily create such an effect by using the optional CELLPADDING attribute in the TABLE tag. CELLPADDING allows you to specify a value in pixels by which all elements within table cells are set off from the edge of the cell. Change the TABLE tag to specify a padding value of 8 pixels:

```
<TABLE WIDTH="100%" BORDER="0" CELLPADDING="8">
```

Figure 12-5 shows the result. Note two things about the CELLPADDING attribute:

- CELLPADDING can be applied only to an entire table, not to individual cells. In Figure 12-5, an 8-pixel padding has been applied to all three cells, with good results.

- Padding is applied to all four sides of a cell.

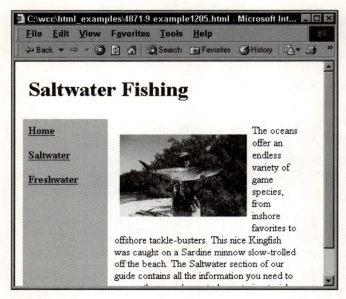

Figure 12-5
A padding of 8 pixels in each table cell greatly improves the appearance of the page.

Using the CELLSPACING attribute

The CELLSPACING attribute is similar to the CELLPADDING attribute. The difference is that instead of adding space between the edges of a cell and the cell's contents, CELLSPACING adds space between cells. The default value for CELLSPACING is 2 pixels. Specify a higher value to add a thicker border between cells:

```
<TABLE BORDER="2" CELLSPACING="8">
```

Figure 12-6 shows two tables. The first one has CELLSPACING set to 8 pixels; the second includes no CELLSPACING attribute and thus has the default spacing of 2 pixels.

Tables can get complicated. If your page doesn't appear the way you want it to and you can't figure out why, temporarily give your tables a border. This makes it easier to troubleshoot and to find where the error lies.

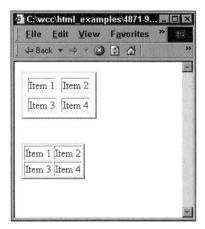

Figure 12-6
The top table has an 8-pixel spacing between cells, and the bottom one has the default 2-pixel spacing. The effect of CELLSPACING is hard to see without borders, so we've given these tables BORDER values of 2 pixels.

Done!

REVIEW

In this session, you have learned to use borderless tables as a page-layout tool. This has included:

- Laying out text in columns
- Understanding limitations of tables for creating columns
- Creating sidebars

QUIZ YOURSELF

1. What attribute and value must be included in a TABLE tag to create a borderless table? (See "Getting Away from the Linear Look.")
2. What is the main reason for using newspaper-style columns? (See "Arranging Text in Columns.")

3. What are two drawbacks to creating newspaper-style columns using tables? (See "Limitations of the Columnar Approach.")

4. What is a sidebar? (See "Creating a Sidebar.")

5. How can you create a margin around the contents of a table cell? (See "Using the CELLPADDING Attribute.")

Using Frames

Session Checklist

✔ Dividing a Web page by using frames

✔ Using frames to create a fixed heading

✔ Creating a fixed sidebar

**30 Min.
To Go**

F rames are yet another way of dividing a Web page into sections or, to put it another way, to combine several individual pages into one. As you have learned in previous sessions, when a particular Web page is too long (or too wide) to fit into a browser window, a vertical (or horizontal) scroll bar appears in the browser; the user can use this scroll bar to reveal the rest of the page. A frame is a section of a Web page that can be scrolled independently of the other sections (frames). For example, if you divide a page into two side-by-side frames, the user can scroll the left section while the right section remains fixed, or vice versa.

A Basic Framed Page

Up to this point, you have worked with Web pages that consist of a single HTML file. It's important to understand that a page that uses frames is made up of several HTML files. Each individual frame consists of a separate HTML file. A *frameset page* specifies the size and positioning of the frames; you can think of it as a master page that combines the individual frames into one Web page. A frameset page contains a FRAMESET tag that defines the frames that make up the page. Listing 13-1 is a frameset page that defines two horizontal frames, one above the other. The HTML file top.html appears in the top frame, and the file bottom.html appears in the bottom frame, as shown in Figure 13-1.

Listing 13-1:

```
<FRAMESET ROWS="50%, 50%">
    <FRAME NAME="top" SRC="top.html">
    <FRAME NAME="bottom" SRC="bottom.html">
</FRAMESET>
```

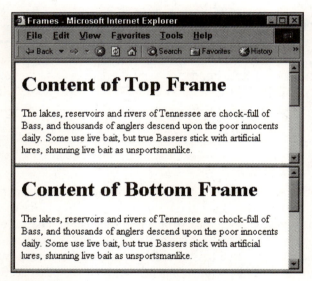

Figure 13-1
A page divided into two frames, each of which can scroll independently of the other

Note the following facts about frames:

- The FRAMESET tag, which is a paired tag (must have a matching ending tag), contains FRAME tags. The content of a FRAME tag is within the tag itself, and it has no corresponding ending tag.

- A frameset page contains no actual content. Content is contained in the files specified in the FRAME tags. A frameset page *does not* include a BODY tag.

- The ROWS attribute creates horizontal frames, and the COLS attribute creates vertical frames (columns).

- Like table cells, the size of a row or column in a frameset may be specified in absolute (pixel) values or in relative (percentage) values.

- Like the IMG tag, a FRAME tag contains an SRC attribute, which specifies a source for the contents of the frame. This must be an existing HTML file. For this example to work, you must create two additional HTML files: top.html and bottom.html.

- Each FRAME has a NAME of your choosing, which you'll use later to refer to the frame.

You don't need to use frames to divide pages into fixed sections. You can do so more efficiently by using tables or style sheets. In general, frames are used when you want a certain section to remain fixed while another section scrolls.

To understand the examples in this section, your files need to include some pretty lengthy text content so that the pages are long enough to have to scroll. The HTML examples on this book's CD-ROM contain the necessary ramblings; the printed examples in the book, for brevity's sake, do not.

Framing a Heading

**20 Min.
To Go**

You've learned two ways to create a main heading for a Web page: by using Heading tags and by using a graphic logo, as in Session 9. An attractive, appropriate logo is something every Web site should have, and it's an important element in reinforcing your brand and your site's identity.

Some Web site owners consider site branding so important that they want their site or organizational logo to appear on every page, in view at all times. With an ordinary Web page, this isn't practical; as soon as the user scrolls down the page, the heading at the top is out of sight. Also, if you want to have the same heading on every page of your site, you must duplicate the code on every page.

Frames to the rescue! If you create a page that has a top and a bottom frame and put the heading in the top frame and everything else in the bottom frame, you can realize several benefits:

- The bottom frame, with the body text, can scroll while the heading remains fixed at the top of the page.

- As the user visits various pages of the site, the heading does not need to reload each time. This saves load time, especially if the heading is a graphic image.
- If you decide to change the heading later, you have to make the change only once.

Here is the code to make this happen (Listing 13-2). The resulting Web page appears in Figure 13-2.

Listing 13-2:

```
<FRAMESET ROWS="80,*">

    <FRAME SRC="heading.html" NAME="top" FRAMEBORDER="0"
        SCROLLING="No" NORESIZE>
    <FRAME SRC="body.html" NAME="bottom" FRAMEBORDER="0"
        SCROLLING="Auto">

</FRAMESET>
```

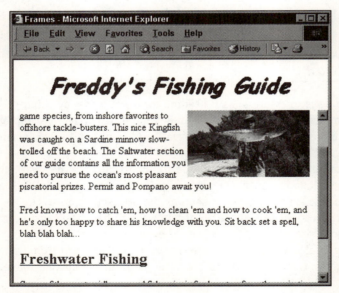

Figure 13-2
A heading contained in a frame. Because the top frame has the SCROLLING="No" and NORESIZE attributes, it is not apparent that the page uses frames at all until you start to scroll the lower section.

To achieve the desired effect, we've added several things to the previous example:

- In the FRAMESET tag, we've specified the height of the first frame as an absolute value of 80 pixels (you may remember that our heading graphic is 60-pixels high). The second value is an asterisk (*), which means that the second frame fills the remaining height of the window.

- Both FRAME tags have the attribute FRAMEBORDER="0", which is why these frames, unlike the ones in the previous example, have no border.

- The upper frame specifies SCROLLING="No", which means that the frame does not scroll. The lower frame specifies SCROLLING="auto", which means that, if the content is too long to fit in the window, scroll bars appear to allow the user to scroll down to the remaining content.

- The upper frame specifies NORESIZE. By default, a user can adjust the relative size of the frames in a page by simply grabbing the frame border and dragging it. The optional NORESIZE attribute prevents the user from doing so.

A*bove the fold* is a quaint expression that has migrated from print media. The portion of a Web page that is visible when the page first loads, without scrolling, is said to be above the fold. It's wise to place your most important content, or whatever you want a visitor to see immediately, above the fold.

**10 Min.
To Go**

Framing a Navbar

In Session 12, we create a sidebar that contains navigational links to the main sections of Freddy's rapidly evolving Web site. This helpful feature is included in one form or another in all well-designed sites and is known as a *navbar*. The idea is that a user, no matter what page he or she visits in a particular site, should be able quickly to find his or her way back to the home page and all of the main site features. Many sites include a navbar on every page.

A navbar can appear on a left or right sidebar or on a *top bar* or *bottom bar*. Many sites have both a side navbar and a bottom navbar, and some complex sites such as search engines and portals even have navbars on all four sides. In Session 20 and Session 22, you learn more about creating an effective and attractive navbar.

Just as you do with a heading in the preceding section, you can create a navbar that remains fixed regardless of what page a user visits or how far down the user scrolls. Instead of dividing the page horizontally, divide it vertically by using the following code (Listing 13-3). Note that we have set SCROLLING="Auto" this time because a navbar frame needs to be free to scroll if necessary. The resulting page is shown in Figure 13-3.

Listing 13-3:

```
<FRAMESET COLS="140,*">

    <FRAME SRC="navbar.html" NAME="left_sidebar" FRAMEBORDER="0"
SCROLLING="Auto" NORESIZE>
    <FRAME SRC="freshwater.html" NAME="right_column"
FRAMEBORDER="0" SCROLLING="Auto">

</FRAMESET>
```

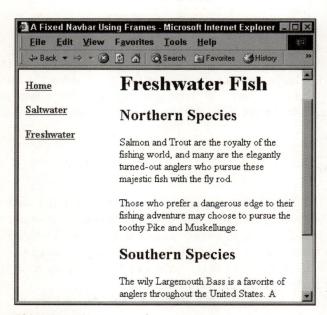

Figure 13-3
Using frames to create a fixed left navbar. Clicking the links on the navbar causes a page to load into the lower-right frame.

In the preceding example, we place a navbar in a left-hand sidebar. If you prefer, you can have a navbar on the right-hand side. Try converting Listing 13-3 to a right-hand sidebar by reversing the order of the two FRAME tags and changing the FRAMESET tag so that it reads <FRAMESET COLS="*,140">. A top bar or bottom bar is also a possibility. If you choose to have a fixed heading at the top of a page (as in Listing 13-2), you may prefer to have your navigational elements at the top, and have no sidebar. To do so, simply add the navigational links to the HTML page that contains the heading.

If all this seems confusing, don't worry. In Session 14, you learn more about frames, including some tips to make sure that your frames always work correctly.

Done!

REVIEW

In this session, you have learned to use frames to create sections of a Web page that scroll independently of one another. This has included:

- Creating a frameset page
- Dividing a page vertically to create a fixed heading
- Dividing a page horizontally to create a fixed sidebar

QUIZ YOURSELF

1. A framed page is made up of several HTML files. What is the master HTML file for the page called, and what tag is its key element? (See "A Basic Framed Page.")
2. What's the main difference between dividing a page by using frames and dividing a page by using tables? (See "A Basic Framed Page.")
3. What are two attributes every FRAME tag should have? (See "A Basic Framed Page.")
4. What is the purpose of the NORESIZE attribute? (See "Framing a Heading.")
5. What is a navbar? (See "Framing a Navbar.")

Advanced Frame Techniques

Session Checklist

✔ Building a functional three-frame page

✔ Using hyperlinks within frames

✔ Avoiding the drawbacks of using frames

**30 Min.
To Go**

In Session 13, you learn to divide a Web page into independently-scrolling sections by using frames. Frames are a powerful tool, but if you use them improperly they can be a detriment to your site rather than an asset; unfortunately, there are many Web sites that fit this description. In this session, you learn several concepts that help you ensure that your framed pages work the way you intend.

In Session 13, we have created a Web page with a fixed heading, and another with a fixed navbar. In this session you learn to combine these techniques to create a page that has both horizontal and vertical frames.

Designing a Three-Frame Page

A single frameset can contain as many frames as you like (although it's rare for a frameset to contain more than two or three frames, as this tends to result in a cramped and cluttered page). Each frameset, however, creates a horizontal *or* a vertical division. In other words, a frameset can create horizontal rows or vertical columns, but not both. If you want to use both horizontal and vertical frames on the same page, you must do so by nesting one frameset inside of another.

For example, you can combine the fixed heading and fixed navbar concepts we discuss in Session 13 simply by nesting two horizontal frames inside the lower vertical frame, as in the following code (Listing 14-1). Note that a FRAMESET can contain FRAMEs or other FRAMESETs:

Listing 14-1:

```
<FRAMESET ROWS="80,*" FRAMEBORDER="0">

    <FRAME SRC="heading.html" NAME="top"
    FRAMEBORDER="0" SCROLLING="No" NORESIZE>

    <FRAMESET COLS="140,*">

        <FRAME SRC="navbar.html" NAME="left_sidebar" FRAMEBORDER="0"
SCROLLING="Auto" NORESIZE>
        <FRAME SRC="freshwater.html" NAME="right_column"
FRAMEBORDER="0" SCROLLING="Auto">

    </FRAMESET>

</FRAMESET>
```

This page layout shown in Figures 14-1 and Figure 14-2 is popular. As we discuss in Session 13, many designers find it desirable that the heading and the navbar remain visible even when the user scrolls to view content lower on the page. Also, this page layout is bandwidth-efficient. As the user navigates to various areas of the site, an HTML file containing only the unique content of each page is loaded into the lower right frame. The heading and navbar, which are often slower-loading graphic elements, don't have to load again for every page.

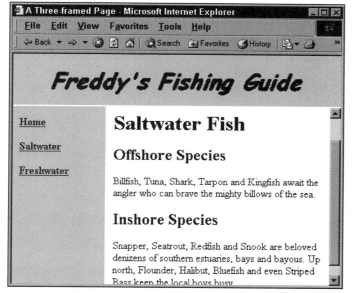

Figure 14-1
This is a typical use of frames. The heading and navbar are fixed. Click the links on the navbar to load the specified file into the lower-right frame. The Saltwater hub page (saltwater.html) is displayed here.

Using Hyperlinks within Frames

Any time you use a hyperlink within a frame, you must include the TARGET attribute in your Anchor tag. The TARGET attribute specifies which frame an HTML file is to be loaded into and is, therefore, an integral part of any page that uses frames. If you don't use the TARGET attribute or if you use it incorrectly, your framed pages may come out a jumbled mess.

In the first part of this session, you use the FRAMESET tag to define a set of frames and give each frame a unique name. Use this name to load an HTML file into the specified frame. On our sidebar, the two links to the Saltwater and Freshwater sections both specify the frame right_column as the target. Clicking one of these links loads the specified file into the right_column frame.

The value of the TARGET attribute can be either the name of an existing frame or one of the following:

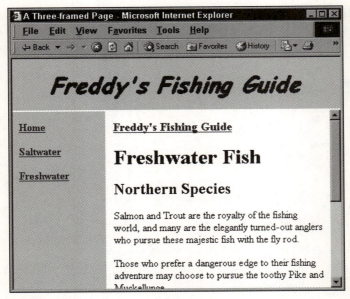

Figure 14-2
Click Freshwater, and freshwater.html appears in the lower-right frame; the heading and navbar remain fixed.

- _blank: opens the linked page in a new browser window
- _parent: opens the linked page in the same browser window but as an individual page without frames
- _top: opens the linked page in the topmost browser window, clearing existing frames
- _self: opens the linked page in the same frame

Any time you link to a page that you *don't* want to appear in a frame, specify a TARGET of _blank, _parent, or _top. On our sidebar, the link called Home specifies TARGET="_parent", so the home page (index.html) opens in a full window, with no frames. In this way, you can combine framed and non-framed pages in a site if you are very careful to set the targets of all hyperlinks correctly. Figure 14-3 shows what a huge mess a tiny error with the TARGET attribute can cause.

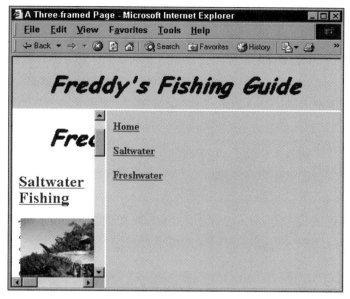

Figure 14-3
*Oops! On a framed site, making a small mistake when you are coding a link
can mean that the user sees a jumbled mess. Make sure every Anchor tag
has the correct TARGET attribute, and be sure to test every link.*

The TARGET attribute has another use that has nothing to do with frames. You
can use TARGET="_blank" any time you want a link to open a page in a new
browser window. For example, some sites use this technique with all off-site links.
Whenever a Web surfer clicks away to some other site, there's a chance that they'll
never find their way back to your site. However, if you specify TARGET="_parent",
the page containing the link remains open, increasing the chance that a user
returns to your site.

The NOFRAMES Tag

**10 Min.
To Go**

Some older browsers don't support frames. The NOFRAMES tag enables you to specify
alternative content to accommodate these users. If a user's browser doesn't support
frames, it should automatically load whatever appears between the beginning and
ending NOFRAMES tags. For example:

```
<NOFRAMES>
```

```
Your browser doesn't support frames. Get a decent browser and come
back later!
</NOFRAMES>
```

Any HTML content can be included between the NOFRAMES tags, so if you wish you can include a complete non-framed version of the page for the benefit of people using old legacy browsers. The NOFRAMES tag must be used within a pair of FRAMESET tags.

 Only three elements can be included between a pair of FRAMESET **tags: a** FRAME, **another nested** FRAMESET, **or a** NOFRAMES **element.**

Disadvantages of Frames

Frames are controversial, not because they are improper HTML but because they have certain inherent disadvantages. Many designers use them, but others avoid them entirely, citing the following drawbacks:

- Lack of support in some earlier browsers.
- Window-size mismatches. You never know what size browser window a particular user may be using. If the window is too small to accommodate one or more of your frames, the frames scroll, which may cause your page to look very unattractive. Or, if you specify SCROLLING="No" as you learn to do earlier in this session, some elements in the frame may be hidden and unavailable.
- Pages loading in the wrong frames. You must be extremely careful that all links have the TARGET attribute set correctly; otherwise, pages may load into the wrong frames, with disastrous results.
- Cramped appearance. Framed pages can have a cramped and a claustrophobic look. Framed pages can force you to try to cram too much information into too small a space.

If you choose to use frames, minimize their drawbacks by following these sound design principles:

- Always use the NOFRAMES tag.
- Be careful about specifying SCROLLING="No". In Listing 14-1, we use it for the heading frame but not for the navbar frame. If a user has a browser

window that's too small to display the entire navbar frame, it can scroll so that the user has access to all the elements on the navbar.

- If you use frames in your site, *every* hyperlink should have the TARGET attribute. Test every link carefully to be sure that pages load the way you intend.

- As a general rule, you should never use more than three frames in a page.

- Every HTML file that opens in a frame should be designed with the frame's size and shape in mind. A page designed to appear full-screen may not look good in a frame.

- As with all Web techniques, you should never use frames unless you have a specific reason for doing so. If you can achieve a desired effect by using tables or style sheets, use them instead of frames.

Never include a page from another site in a frame on your own site for two reasons: first, it's bad design, as a page designed to appear on its own may not look right in a frame. Second (unless you have permission from the site owner), it constitutes copyright infringement, which is unethical and illegal. Any time you link to another Web site, specify a TARGET **value of** _blank **,** _parent, **or** _top, **so that the link opens in its own browser window.**

REVIEW

In this session, you have learned some of the finer points of using frames:

Done!

- Creating a three-section page that has a top heading and side navbar
- Using links in frames
- Recognizing and avoiding the drawbacks of frames

QUIZ YOURSELF

1. How do you create a framed page that has both a fixed top heading and a fixed sidebar? (See "Designing a Three-Frame Page.")

2. What attribute of the Anchor tag should always be used when a hyperlink occurs within a frame? (See "Using Hyperlinks within Frames.")

3. What are the four possible special values of the TARGET attribute? (See "Using Hyperlinks within Frames.")

4. What is the purpose of the NOFRAMES tag? (See "The NOFRAMES Tag.")

5. What is a good maximum number of frames for a Web page? (See "Disadvantages of Frames.")

Enabling User Feedback

Session Checklist

✔ Creating an e-mail link

✔ Using forms to enable user input

✔ Creating various types of form input fields

**30 Min.
To Go**

O ne of the most compelling things about the Web, and one of the features that sets it apart from other media, is its potential for instant user feedback. In this session, you learn to offer your site users ways to communicate with you, the site owner.

A Simple E-mail Link

You can easily enable site users to contact you by e-mail by creating a *mailto* hyperlink, which has the following format:

```
<A HREF="mailto:fred@fredsfishingguide.com">Click here to send an
email to Fred</A>.
```

This works just like a hyperlink to a Web page except that instead of a Web address, it contains the code `mailto:` followed by an e-mail address. Like the links you are familiar with, a mailto hyperlink can be wrapped around any text or image and is highlighted according to browser defaults.

When the user clicks this link, whatever e-mail software is installed on his or her system as the default e-mail client pops up; a new message is created, addressed to Fred.

The way you present your contact information is extremely important. It's a large factor in the image that your Web site presents; if you are running a business Web site, your presentation of contact information has a major effect on the number of customers your site attracts. Therefore, be sure to stick to the following sound principles:

- Every Web site should provide a way to contact the site owner by e-mail. This contact link should be easy for users to find. Many sites choose to include such a link on their main navbar, which appears on every page of the site.

- Every business Web site needs to provide a telephone number and a street address. Savvy Web users consider the lack of a street address a sign of a fly-by-night business.

- A business e-mail address should use the business's unique domain name (that is, the same domain name used by the Web site). For example, `fred@fredsfishingguide.com` sounds more professional and is easier to remember than `fred@aol.com` or `fred@hotmail.com`. Establishing such an address is done by means of an *e-mail alias*, which is configured on your hosting service's mail server. When someone sends a message to `you@YourDomainName.com`, the mail server redirects it to your existing e-mail address. Any decent hosting service can set up one or more e-mail aliases for you on request.

- Usually, larger organizations make several e-mail addresses available for different types of inquiries. For example, you might ask users to contact `sales@fredsfishingguide.com` for sales inquiries, `fred@fredsfishingguide.com` for personal inquiries to Fred himself, and `webmaster@fredsfishingguide.com` for comments about the Web site. E-mail aliases direct these addresses to the appropriate people.

- On more complex sites, the contact link on the navbar leads to a separate page of contact information that contains various e-mail addresses, phone and fax numbers, mailing addresses, and so on. This page may also include answers to *frequently asked questions* (FAQs) so that many users can find the answers they're looking for without having to send an e-mail message. In addition, the site owners don't have to spend time answering the same questions over and over.

- Simple sites such as Fred's may have the contact link on the navbar lead directly to a mailto link, with no separate contact page.

20 Min. To Go

Managing Feedback by Using Forms

HTML forms enable you to solicit information from your users in a precise and customized way. You can tell your users what information you want and can ensure that it is submitted to you in a predefined format. Forms have many uses:

- Sorting and standardizing e-mail feedback
- Enabling user registration
- Conducting user surveys
- Online ordering of products or services

Using the FORM tag

An online form is contained within a pair of FORM tags, as in Listing 15-1. Figure 15-1 shows the Web page created by this code:

Listing 15-1:

```
<FORM ACTION="mailto:fred@fredsfishingguide.com" METHOD="post">

<INPUT TYPE="text" NAME="Name" SIZE="15">
Name

<INPUT TYPE="text" NAME="Address" SIZE="15">
Address

<INPUT TYPE="submit" VALUE="Submit">

</FORM>
```

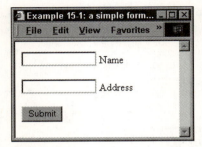

Figure 15-1
A simple form with two text entry boxes and a Submit button.

Note the following facts about the FORM element:

- The ACTION attribute specifies a URL to which the browser sends the information that the user enters in the form, in this example an e-mail address.

- The FORM tag is used in pairs (that is, it must have both opening and closing tags), with one or more INPUT tags (described in the next section) or other tags contained between the FORM tags.

- FORMs cannot be nested (that is, a FORM cannot be contained within another FORM), but FORMs can contain other elements or be contained by them. For example, a FORM can be included in a table cell, and a FORM can include all the usual formatting tags such as Paragraphs, Lists, and so on.

**10 Min.
To Go**

Creating input fields

An online form enables a user to enter data on a Web page in much the same way that one enters data in a desktop application. Different types of input fields are appropriate for different types of data, so there are several possibilities, any combination of which can be included between two FORM tags to make up a form.

The INPUT element

The INPUT element creates a single field into which a user can enter data.

```
<INPUT TYPE="text" NAME="Name" SIZE="15">
```

This example creates a text input box 15-characters wide. Every INPUT must have a NAME of your choosing. The TYPE attribute specifies one of several possible types of input fields, and the optional SIZE attribute sets the size of the field on the Web page. The text box is just one of several valid input types:

- CHECKBOX. For those yes-or-no questions
- RADIO. For questions requiring a choice among two or more possible answers
- RESET. A button that resets the user-entered values to their default values
- SUBMIT. A button that submits the form (that is, sends the user-entered data to the URL specified in the FORM tag)

Listing 15-2 is an example of a form containing several different types of INPUT elements, and Figure 15-2 shows the resulting Web page.

Listing 15-2:

```
<FORM ACTION="mailto:fred@fredsfishingguide.com" METHOD="post">

<INPUT TYPE="text" NAME="Name" SIZE="15">
<STRONG>Text Box</STRONG>
<P>
<INPUT TYPE="checkbox" NAME="Checkbox" VALUE="Yes" CHECKED>
<STRONG>Checkbox</STRONG>
<P>
<STRONG>Radio Buttons:</STRONG>
<BR>
<INPUT TYPE="radio" NAME="RadioButton" VALUE="Option A" CHECKED>
Option A
<INPUT TYPE="radio" NAME="RadioButton" VALUE="Option B">
Option B
<INPUT TYPE="radio" NAME="RadioButton" VALUE="Option C">
Option C

</FORM>
```

The SELECT and OPTION elements

The SELECT element allows the user to select one or more options from a list, with each option represented by an OPTION tag. Listing 15-3 is a basic application; the result is shown in Figure 15-3.

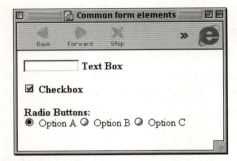

Figure 15-2
The INPUT tag can take several different values for the TYPE attribute, offering several different types of input fields.

Listing 15-3:

```
<STRONG>Select one or more of the following options:</STRONG>
<BR><BR>
<SELECT NAME="Favorite" SIZE="3" MULTIPLE>
     <OPTION VALUE="one">Option One</OPTION>
     <OPTION VALUE="two">Option No. 2</OPTION>
     <OPTION VALUE="three">Option Three</OPTION>
</SELECT>
```

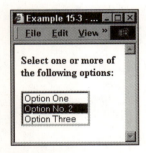

Figure 15-3
Use the SELECT and OPTION elements to let users choose from a list of options. By default, users can select only one of the available options; in this case users can select multiple options because the tag includes the MULTIPLE attribute.

The TEXTAREA tag

The text input box you have created by using the INPUT tag allows users to enter only one line of text. For multiple-line messages, use TEXTAREA. The ROWS and COLS attributes set the vertical size and horizontal size of the text box, respectively, as in Listing 15-4. Figure 15-4 shows the resulting page.

Listing 15-4:

```
<STRONG>Tell your story below:</STRONG>
<BR><BR>
<TEXTAREA COLS="32" ROWS="6" NAME="comments">
Enter text here.
</TEXTAREA>
```

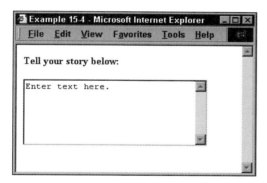

Figure 15-4
A TEXTAREA Box. Note that the text between the TEXTAREA tags appears by default.

Done!

REVIEW

In this session, you have learned to enable Web-page users to send feedback by:

- Creating a simple e-mail link
- Creating forms to enable user input
- Appropriate input elements for different types of data

QUIZ YOURSELF

1. A hyperlink that sends an e-mail message can be created using the Anchor (A) tag. What must the target of the link be for this to work? (See "A Simple E-mail Link.")

2. What are some common uses of forms? (See "Managing Feedback by Using Forms.")

3. What does the ACTION attribute of the FORM tag specify? (See "Using the FORM tag.")

4. The INPUT tag can present any of several input field types to the user. Name three types. (See "Creating Input Fields.")

5. Name three tags other than the INPUT tag that can be used to present user input fields. (See "Creating Input Fields.")

Building Interactive Forms

Session Checklist

✔ Creating a survey by using various form input elements

✔ Processing user input

✔ Activating a script from a form

**30 Min.
To Go**

I n Session 16, you learn to create online forms, which enable Web site users to submit information to you, the site owner. In this session, we discuss a couple of practical examples in which you might solicit information from users, as well as some ways to process the information you receive.

A User Survey

It can be very valuable to know a bit about your site users and what sort of content they are interested in; one way to gather this information is to invite users to fill out a survey. Throughout this book, we've been building an example Web site called Fred's Fishing Guide. Listing 16-1 is a simple survey for Fred's site users, including examples of most of the form elements discussed in Session 15. We've included the form elements in a table to make them line up neatly on the page.

Listing 16-1:

```
<H1>Fred's User Survey</H1>
<P>Hey, fish fans! Fill in the blanks, and hit the Submit button!
<P>
<FORM ACTION="mailto:fred@fredsfishingguide.com" METHOD="post">
<TABLE WIDTH="100%" CELLSPACING="2" CELLPADDING="10" BORDER="0">
<TR>
   <TD WIDTH="50%">
   <INPUT TYPE="text" NAME="Name" SIZE="15">
<STRONG>Name</STRONG>
   </TD>
   <TD WIDTH="50%">
   <INPUT TYPE="text" NAME="Address" SIZE="15">
<STRONG>Email</STRONG>
   </TD>
</TR>
<TR>
   <TD WIDTH="50%" VALIGN="top">
   <STRONG>Favorite type of fishing?</STRONG>
   <SELECT NAME="Favorite" SIZE="4" MULTIPLE>
      <OPTION VALUE="fly">Fly Fishing</OPTION>
      <OPTION VALUE="bass">Bass Fishing</OPTION>
      <OPTION VALUE="offshore">Offshore Trolling</OPTION>
      <OPTION VALUE="inshore">Inshore Saltwater</OPTION>
   </SELECT>
   </TD>
   <TD WIDTH="50%" VALIGN="top">
   <STRONG>How do you like Fred's?</STRONG>
   <BR>
   <INPUT TYPE="radio" NAME="Opinion" VALUE="Good" CHECKED>
   It's good.
   <BR>
   <INPUT TYPE="radio" NAME="Opinion" VALUE="Bad">
   It's bad.
   </TD>
</TR>
<TR>
   <TD COLSPAN="2">
   <INPUT TYPE="checkbox" NAME="AddtoList" VALUE="Yes" CHECKED>
<STRONG>Add me to Fred's email list.</STRONG>
```

```
    </TD>
  </TR>
  <TR>
    <TD WIDTH="50%">
    <INPUT TYPE="submit" VALUE="Submit to Fred">
    </TD>
    <TD WIDTH="50%">
    <INPUT TYPE="reset" VALUE="Reset Form">
    </TD>
  </TR>
</TABLE>
</FORM>
```

In Session 15, you learn that you can combine form elements with other elements such as Paragraph tags, tables and so forth. Getting form elements to line up neatly can be a challenge; often, the best solution is to include them in a table, as we do in Listing 16-1. We've used a table to create two columns (but note that the line that invites users to join Freddy's mailing list spans both columns, because we've specified COLSPAN="2"). Remember that all the elements that make up a form *must* be included between a pair of FORM tags.

Figure 16-1 shows the resulting online form, partially filled in by a fishing fan.

Processing User Input

**20 Min.
To Go**

The purpose of a form is to allow site users to send information to the site owner, but how does this happen exactly? When a user clicks the Submit button, a set of *name/value pairs* is sent to the address specified in the ACTION attribute of the FORM tag.

You learn in Session 15 that each input element of a form (including INPUT, SELECT and TEXTAREA tags) must have a unique name, which you assign by using the NAME attribute. Whatever value the user enters into a particular input element (input field) becomes the value associated with that element's name. For example, the set of name/value pairs the form generates in Listing 16-1 might be:

Name = Billy Bass
Address = billybass@billybass.com
Favorite = fly
Opinion = Good
AddtoList = Yes

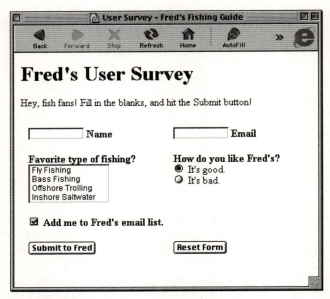

Figure 16-1
*Different input elements are appropriate for different types of data. This
user survey employs several input elements. We've used a table to arrange
the form elements into two columns.*

Note that some types of input elements, such as the text box, allow the user to
type any value; other input elements, such as the radio buttons and checkbox,
allow the user to select only from among values you (the site designer) specify.

To understand how a form sends user data in the form of name/value pairs, go
through the following steps:

1. Launch your Web editor, and open the file containing Freddy's user survey
   from the accompanying CD-ROM (`freds_fishing_guide/survey.html`).
   This is the same as Listing 16-1.

2. Change the FORM tag, replacing Fred's e-mail address with your own, as
   follows:

   ```
   <FORM ACTION="mailto:YourEmailAddress@Whatever.com"
   METHOD="post">
   ```

3. Save the file under a new name on your hard drive, and open it in a Web
   browser. You should see a page similar to Figure 16-1.

4. Take the survey, filling in each of the fields with your own information.
   Click the Submit button. The browser sends the data you have just
   entered to your e-mail address (you must be connected to the Internet
   at this point).

5. Wait a minute; then launch your e-mail client and check your e-mail. You should have a new message containing the data.

6. Depending on your system, the data may be in the form of an attached file rather than in the body of the message. If so, open the attached file by using Notepad or another word processor.

7. You should see something like this:

```
Name=Billy+Bass&Address=billybass@billybass.com
&Favorite=bass&Opinion=Good&AddtoList=Yes
```

8. Replace each ampersand (&) with a line break, and you should see basically the same list of name/value pairs described previously in this session:

```
Name=Billy+Bass
Address=billybass@billybass.com
Favorite=bass
Opinion=Good
AddtoList=Yes
```

Of course, what you do with this data once you receive it is up to you. Freddy might use it to add Billy Bass to his mailing list, since he now has both Mr. Bass's permission to do so and his e-mail address. Or Freddy might save all the responses from the survey for a month, count how many users choose each type of fishing as their favorite, and plan future site content accordingly.

**10 Min.
To Go**

A User Feedback Form

In the previous session you learn to enable users to send e-mail to a site owner or *Webmaster* (a Webmaster is the person responsible for maintaining a site) by means of a simple mailto link. This is effective, but you can exert more control over your incoming e-mail by having users send messages indirectly through a form.

The user survey you've created earlier in this session is a feedback form that allows users to answer specific questions. By adding a TEXTAREA box to a feedback form, you can enable users to send you comments of any length. Of course, you can do the same with a simple mailto link, but the advantage of using a form is that you can ask users for specific information in addition to free-form comments.

Listing 16-2 is a simple feedback form. It asks users to supply their names and e-mail addresses, as well as the nature of their inquiries. The user must choose one of three possible subjects, so Freddy can sort his incoming email into three categories. If Subject=sales, Freddy forwards the message to his sales department. If Subject=complaint, it goes in the trash. Figure 16-2 shows how the feedback form looks on the page. As in Listing 16-1, we've used a table to make the form elements line up, but in Listing 16-2, we omit the table tags for clarity.

Listing 16-2:

```
<FORM ACTION="mailto:fred@fredsfishingguide.com" METHOD="post">

<INPUT NAME="Name" SIZE="15">
Name

<INPUT NAME="Address" SIZE="15">
Email

What's this about?
<BR>

<INPUT TYPE="radio" NAME="Subject" VALUE="fishing" CHECKED>
Fishing
  

<INPUT TYPE="radio" NAME="Subject" VALUE="complaint">
Complaint
  

<INPUT TYPE="radio" NAME="Subject" VALUE="sales">
Sales

<TEXTAREA COLS="32" ROWS="6" NAME="comments">
User can enter text here.
</TEXTAREA>

<INPUT TYPE="submit" VALUE="Submit to Fred">

<INPUT TYPE="reset" VALUE="Reset Form">

</FORM>
```

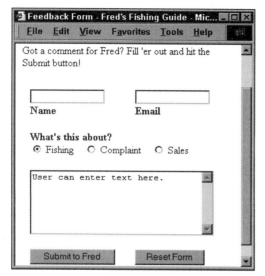

Figure 16-2
Some sites prefer to enable user feedback through a form such as the one here rather than by using a direct e-mail link.

About CGI Scripts

Previously in this session, you create a page that enables a user to send you data by e-mail. However, deciphering this data manually, to say nothing of doing something with it, is tedious. For a Web site with a large number of user submissions, deciphering this data manually becomes almost impossible. As you may have guessed, most online forms are not designed to send data directly to a human but to a computer program. A *program* can receive input, process data, and deliver output, something that HTML cannot do on its own. Processing user data over the Internet is often done by a type of program called a *script*.

Scripts can be written to do almost any kind of data-processing task, and over the years thousands of scripts have been written for use on Web sites. Some are commercial products, but some are available free from various resource sites such as ScriptSearch (http://scriptsearch.internet.com/). Most hosting services also have a library of scripts available for use on customer sites.

Scripts automate the task of deciphering and interpreting the data users send by using forms. Previously in this session, we imagine poor Freddy sifting through all the responses to his question about users' favorite types of fishing. Fortunately for him, a simple script can automatically keep a running total of his users' preferences.

Traditionally, a form sends data to a *Common Gateway Interface (CGI) script*. CGI is not a computer language but a specification for transferring information between a Web page and a CGI program. The program itself can be written in just about any language, although Perl is perhaps the most popular.

The two examples of forms for user feedback in this session are common front ends for CGI scripts. Lots of user-survey scripts and mailing-form scripts are available. To send the input from a form to a script, simply specify the script's name and location in the FORM tag:

```
<FORM ACTION="http://FredsHostingService.net/
cgi-bin/user_survey.cgi" METHOD="post">
```

Note that the CGI script has a `.cgi` file extension and (usually) resides in a directory called `cgi-bin`.

Note

Because scripts are actual programs that run on a server, they represent a potential security risk for a hosting service. That's why ISPs keep all CGI scripts in a special directory (usually called `cgi-bin`**) and guard access to this directory carefully. Most ISPs won't let you put scripts on their server unless they've checked the scripts for security risks. This is one argument in favor of using a hosting service's existing library of scripts instead of rolling your own.**

If you need a script for processing user feedback, you have four options:

1. Write a script yourself in Perl or in some other language. This option is not for the casual Web developer. It takes some programming skill to create good scripts, and many high-quality existing scripts are available anyway.

2. Download a suitable script from a resource Web site such as ScriptSearch (`http://scriptsearch.internet.com/`), and modify it to fit your purposes. Any script you obtain needs to be modified a bit, if only to add your own URLs, variable names, and so on. This usually requires only a little knowledge of scripting. However, this option requires access to your host's `cgi-bin` directory.

3. Use one of the scripts your hosting service provides. This is usually the simplest option. You avoid the security issue, and your hosting service can explain how to get the script to work on your site. Most hosting

services have a good library of CGI scripts: mailto scripts, surveys, search engines, traffic reporting, and more.

4. Bypass CGI and use one of the modern scripting applications such as Microsoft's Active Server Pages (ASP), Java Server Pages (JSP), PHP, or Allaire's ColdFusion. These offer advanced features and a more intuitive, Windows-like programming environment. They also tend to be far more bandwidth-efficient than the old standby CGI-Perl combination. A good hosting service should provide one or more of these handy scripting environments for your use.

Done!

REVIEW

In this session, you have learned to create forms for user feedback and have looked at several ways to process that feedback. This has included:

- Using form input elements to create a user survey
- Receiving user input by e-mail
- Processing user input by using scripts

QUIZ YOURSELF

1. What is one way to get form elements to line up neatly on a page? (See "A User Survey.")

2. What type of data is sent when a user submits a form? (See "Processing User Input.")

3. What attribute determines where this data is sent? (See "Processing User Input.")

4. What are two possible destinations for this data? (See "About CGI Scripts.")

5. Why are ISPs cautious about letting clients put CGI scripts on their servers? (See "About CGI Scripts.")

PART

III

Saturday Afternoon

1. What attribute do you use to set the width of a table or a table cell?

2. In what two ways can you express the width of a table or a table cell?

3. How can you center elements within a table cell?

4. How can you create a horizontal heading spanning several table cells?

5. How can you create a borderless table?

6. Why are newspaper-style columns widely used in print media?

7. What is a sidebar?

8. How is a margin around the contents of a table cell created?

9. A page that uses frames is made up of several HTML files. What do you call the master file for a framed page, and what tag is its main element?

10. Tables and frames can both be used to divide a page. What's the main difference?

11. Name two attributes every FRAME tag should have.

12. What does the NORESIZE attribute do?

13. What is a navbar?

14. When a hyperlink occurs within a frame, what attribute must you include in the Anchor tag?

15. What are four possible values of this attribute?

16. How do you create a hyperlink that sends an e-mail message?

17. What is specified by the ACTION attribute of the FORM tag?

18. Name three tags other than the INPUT tag that can be used to present user-input fields.

19. If you want to offer users a choice between two options on a form, what sort of input element might you use?

20. Most ISPs are cautious about letting clients put CGI scripts on their servers. Why?

PART

IV

Saturday Evening

Controlling Presentation with Cascading Style Sheets

Session Checklist

✔ Applying styles to text

✔ Creating a basic style sheet

✔ Setting styles globally for a Web site

**30 Min.
To Go**

You may remember that in Session 1 we discuss the concept of separating content from its organization and presentation. One way to achieve this goal is to specify the formatting of a document (for example, the size of text, the typeface, color and so on) in a separate document called a *style sheet*, rather than within the document itself. Style sheets are used in many types of media. The style sheets that are used in Web design are based on a technology called Cascading Style Sheets (CSS), which you use in conjunction with HTML.

Styling Text by Using CSS

By now, you've become used to using a number of HTML tags. Many of them specify only the organization of a document. For example, the Heading and Paragraph tags make the relationship between these two elements clear, but they don't specify exactly what styling is to be applied to the elements. What makes a heading? Larger text, bold text, a different font, a different color? The H1 through H6 tags leave it up to the browser to decide.

Other tags, such as the FONT tag, do specify exactly how text is to be presented. For example,

```
<FONT SIZE="4" COLOR="#000080" FACE="Verdana, Arial, Helvetica,
sans-serif">Freddy's Fishing Guide</FONT>
```

This causes the text to be displayed large, light blue, and in a sans-serif font.

Using the FONT tag (or any other tag that applies styles to individual elements) is, as you may have noticed by now, repetitious and tedious. Let's say you want your headings to use a sans-serif font and your body text to use a serif font. This means every heading, and every block of text, needs its own set of FONT tags. Not only does this make your HTML files longer; it multiplies the possibility of mistakes and means that making changes is a major project.

Fortunately, a much more powerful tool enables you to define a desired style for each HTML tag, throughout a document or even an entire site. This important tool is called Cascading Style Sheets (CSS).

For a quick idea of how CSS works, go through the following steps:

1. Open freds_fishing_guide/index.html or another appropriate example file in your HTML editor or word processor.

2. If you've added any FONT tags to this file, get rid of them.

3. Insert the following code in the HEAD section of your document (between the HEAD tags):

```
<STYLE>
H1 { color: blue }
</STYLE>
```

4. Save the file, and view it in a Web browser. All H1 elements are now blue.

Before creating a complete style sheet for Freddy's home page, take a closer look at the parts of a style sheet. A style sheet consists of rules that define how the content of an HTML document is to be presented. The style sheet in the previous example consists of a single rule, which states that all first-level headings (H1) are to be blue. Note the following facts about CSS rules:

- A rule consists of a *selector*, which is the name of an HTML element, followed by a *declaration*, which specifies the styling to be applied to that element. In the preceding example, H1 is the selector, and `color: blue` is the declaration.

- The declaration is enclosed within curly braces.

- A declaration consists of a *property* and a *value* separated by a colon. In the preceding example, `color` is the property and `blue` is the value.

- A rule can contain multiple selectors, separated by commas, and multiple declarations, separated by semicolons.

**20 Min.
To Go**

A Simple Style Sheet

Freddy has decided that he wants all headings on his site to be blue and to use a sans-serif font. He wants all paragraph text to be black and to use a serif font. These design rules can be expressed as a simple style sheet, as shown in Listing 17-1:

Listing 17-1:

```
<STYLE>
H1, H2, H3, H4 {
    color: blue;
    font-family: Verdana, Arial, Helvetica, sans-serif;
    }
P {
    font-family: Garamond, Times, serif;
    }
</STYLE>
```

This style sheet consists of two rules. The first rule specifies a color and preferred font for the H1 through H4 tags. The second rule specifies a preferred font for all text following a P tag. If we add this STYLE element to the HEAD section of `freds_fishing_guide/index.html`, the rules are applied to that file; the result is shown in Figure 17-1.

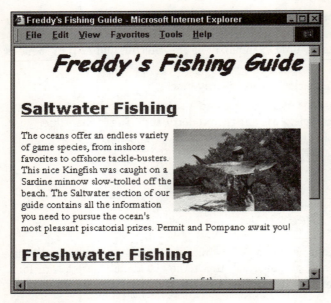

Figure 17-1
Freddy's home page now has headings in Verdana and paragraph text in Garamond, as specified by the style sheet contained in the HEAD section of the document.

Note the following points about CSS:

- The syntax is different from that used within HTML tags. Do not use quotation marks, but be careful to use commas, colons, and semicolons correctly.

- The list of desired fonts is just like the one you learn to create in Session 6. (You see that the FONT tag has been good for something after all!)

- Any property that isn't specified by a style sheet is displayed according to browser defaults. Thus, it isn't necessary to specify black as the color for paragraph text.

**10 Min.
To Go**

Linking to a Style Sheet

In the previous example, we include a style sheet in the HEAD section of a document by using the STYLE tag. This is only one of three ways that style sheets can be applied:

1. Apply styles to an individual element by using the STYLE attribute within a tag.
2. Apply styles to an entire HTML document by including STYLE tags within the HEAD section.
3. Apply styles to a group of documents by creating a master style sheet and including a link to that style sheet in each document.

The first method can be used to apply styles "on the fly" to any HTML element. In this example, the text in the first paragraph is blue.

```
<P STYLE="color:blue">This paragaph is blue.</P>

<P>This paragraph is normal.</P>
```

This method is seldom used, as it defeats one of the main purposes of CSS: reducing repetition and tedium by using a single style sheet for an entire Web site.

The second method, which you apply in Listing 17-1, is a useful tool for learning how style sheets work, but the third method maximizes the benefits of CSS. Using a single style sheet for an entire Web site has the following advantages:

- It minimizes the size of each HTML file, which makes it faster to load and easier to edit.
- It enforces consistent formatting throughout a site, which is a sound design principle.
- It makes it easy to make global changes to a site.

To create a style sheet for Freddy's Fishing Guide, follow these steps:

1. Launch your HTML editor or word processor, and start a new document.
2. Enter the following code (the same as the example earlier in this session, but without the STYLE tags):

```
H1, H2, H3, H4 {
    color: blue;
    font-family: Verdana, Arial, Helvetica, sans-serif;
    }
P   {
    font-family: Garamond, Times, serif;
    }
```

3. Make sure the file contains only the preceding code (no HTML, BODY or other HTML tags).

4. Save the file as a plain text file, giving it the name `style_sheet.css`. Be sure to save it in the same directory as `index.html` and the rest of the HTML files that make up the site. This file is the style sheet for your site.

5. Open `index.html`; remove the STYLE element you have added to the HEAD section in the previous example, and replace it with this code:

```
<LINK REL="stylesheet" HREF="style_sheet.css">
```

This LINK tag establishes a link to the style sheet so that the style sheet `style_sheet.css` is applied to this HTML document.

6. Repeat the previous step to add the link to the style sheet to all the other HTML pages of the site. Make sure that all pages are free of FONT tags. Any formatting applied using FONT tags will override the formatting specified by the style sheet.

This style sheet now controls the text formatting for the entire site. As shown in Figure 17-2, the Saltwater hub page now has the same text styles as the home page. If you want to try an alternative design scheme, simply change the style sheet.

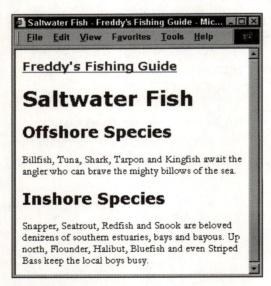

Figure 17-2
Thanks to a very simple style sheet, the browser displays headings in a sans-serif font and paragraph text in a serif font throughout Freddy's site.

Done!

REVIEW

In this session, you have encountered Cascading Style Sheets, a far more powerful tool for arranging and formatting Web-page content than any tool you've used so far. You have learned:

- To apply styles to text elements
- To understand the components of a simple style sheet
- To apply a style sheet to an entire site, using the LINK tag

QUIZ YOURSELF

1. What are the two parts of a CSS rule? (See "Styling Text by Using CSS.")
2. What are the two parts of a CSS declaration? (See "Styling Text by Using CSS.")
3. What determines how a particular property is displayed if that property is not mentioned in a style sheet? (See "A Simple Style Sheet.")
4. What are three ways to apply a style sheet to a document? (See "Linking to a Style Sheet.")
5. What tag is used to apply a style sheet to a group of HTML documents? (See "Linking to a Style Sheet.")

Session Checklist

✔ Making your style sheets trouble-free

✔ Overriding a global style with an inline style

✔ Creating custom styles using classes

**30 Min.
To Go**

I n Session 17, you learn to apply some simple text formatting by using CSS. This scratches the surface of what you can do with style sheets. In this session, you learn several more sophisticated techniques, as well as some ways to ensure that your style sheets work the way you want them to.

Creating Trouble-free Style Sheets

In Session 17, we create a simple style sheet that contains two rules. The first rule specifies that all headings are blue and use a sans-serif font:

```
H1, H2, H3, H4 {
    color: blue;
    font-family: Verdana, Arial, Helvetica, sans-serif;
    }
```

Actually, we've applied this rule to headings H1 through H4 only; Freddy's site doesn't use the H5 or H6 tags, so we can safely leave them out.

The second rule specifies a serif font for all paragraph text:

```
P {
    font-family: Garamond, Times, serif;
}
```

This rule applies to all text that follows a Paragraph (P) tag. But what about text that doesn't have a P tag in front of it?

So that we can more clearly see the difference between styled and nonstyled text, let's say that Freddy has changed his mind. He now wants Verdana text for body text as well as for headings. Thanks to CSS, this change is easy to make. Simply open style_sheet.css, and change the rule for the P tag as follows:

```
P {
    font-family: Verdana, Arial, Helvetica, sans-serif;
}
```

Now open the file freshwaterB.html. This page has a list that the UL and LI elements define, as shown in Listing 18-1:

Listing 18-1:

```
<P>Those who prefer a dangerous edge to their fishing adventure
may choose to pursue the toothy species:
    <UL>
        <LI>Northern Pike
        <LI>Chain Pickerel
        <LI>Muskellunge
    </UL>
```

You learn to create lists in Session 5.

Figure 18-1 shows the page. The headings and the paragraph text have the desired sans-serif font. The list elements, because a P tag does not precede them, do not. They've reverted to the browser default, which is a serif font.

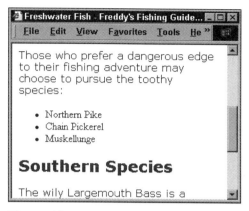

Figure 18-1
The style sheet we've written affects only the Heading and Paragraph tags.
The list elements are in the wrong font because they have no Paragraph tags.

There are three ways to deal with this situation:

1. Use a P tag for all body text. For example, if the list can be rendered thus, it looks fine:

   ```
   <UL>
       <LI><P>Northern Pike
       <LI><P>Chain Pickerel
       <LI><P>Muskellunge
   </UL>
   ```

   This is not an ideal solution; it clutters your code, and there may be certain situations in which you don't want a P tag.

2. You can apply styles to all elements simply by including the BODY tag in a CSS rule. For example:

   ```
   BODY {font-family: Verdana, Arial, Helvetica, sans-serif;}
   ```

   This causes all text on the page to use the specified font. This doesn't work with some legacy browsers, however.

3. You can include all possible text elements as selectors in a CSS rule. For example:

   ```
   P, TR, TD, OL, UL, BLOCKQUOTE, BR {font-family: Verdana, Arial,
   Helvetica, sans-serif;}
   ```

   This causes all these text elements to use the specified font. Other text elements exist, but these are the only ones used on Fred's site.

Style sheets are a relatively recent development, and older legacy browsers (for example, versions of Netscape or Internet Explorer prior to 4.0) may have problems displaying them. Following the procedures outlined in this session should help to minimize such problems.

If Fred decides to go with Verdana font all the way, his style sheet might look like this:

```
BODY    {
    font-family: Verdana, Arial, Helvetica, sans-serif;
        }
H1, H2, H3, H4
        {
    color: blue;
        }
```

The first rule causes all text, including headings, to use Verdana or a sans-serif font. The second rule causes only the headings to be blue.

If Fred goes back to his original plan, with sans-serif for headings and serif for body text, then his style sheet should be:

```
P, TR, TD, OL, UL, BLOCKQUOTE, BR
    {
    font-family: Garamond, Times, serif;
    }

H1, H2, H3, H4
    {
    color: blue;
    font-family: Verdana, Arial, Helvetica, sans-serif;
    }
```

This is a common way of coding style sheets, with each rule and each curly bracket on its own line. Of course, such line breaks and indents don't affect the results of the code; however, they make the code more readable.

Using Inline Styles

So far, you've created style sheets in which a single HTML element has a single style applied to it wherever it appears. For more complex documents, this soon becomes limiting. What if you need to apply a different style to one particular section? For example, let's say you want to show the reader the difference between two fonts. Your site-wide style sheet specifies that all body text is set in a serif font, but you want to display a single line in sans-serif as an example.

The simplest way to do this is to add an inline style to the text element you want to appear differently, as shown in Listing 18-2 (see Figure 18-2):

Listing 18-2:

```
<P>This paragraph uses a serif font, as specified in the site's
style sheet.

<P STYLE="font-family: sans-serif;">This paragraph uses sans-
serif, because the global style sheet is overridden by the inline
style in this Paragraph tag.
```

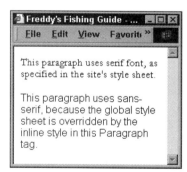

Figure 18-2
The first paragraph uses a serif font, but the second paragraph uses a sans-serif font because its P tag includes an inline style that overrides the document-wide style.

But isn't there a conflict here? The global style sheet says one thing, and the inline style says another. Which styling takes precedence? The hierarchy is as follows:

1. Inline styles (applied by using the STYLE attribute within an HTML tag)

2. Document-wide styles (applied by using the STYLE tag in the HEAD section of a document)

3. Linked style sheets (contained in a .css file and linked to a document by using the LINK tag)

This is why style sheets are referred to as *cascading*. Several style sheets can apply to a particular element, but the more specific style sheet always overrides the more general. If you need to single out a section for special styling, you can apply an inline style to it.

10 Min. To Go

Creating Custom Styles

However, what if you have a recurring text element you want to style in a special way? After all, most books and magazines use many different types of text styles, not just headings and paragraph text. Text elements such as sidebars, captions, author credits, tables of contents, summaries and so on should all have unique styles. You can accomplish this by creating a *class* for each of these elements.

You define a class in a style sheet, specifying the styling to be applied to members of the class. Then by simply including the CLASS attribute in a tag, you can cause that tag to apply the styling you have specified for the class. The CLASS attribute can be included in any HTML tag, and a class can be as simple or as complex as you like. It's a bit like being able to create your own custom tags.

Listing 18-3 shows a paragraph that will be styled according to the class epigraph.

Listing 18-3:

```
<P CLASS="epigraph">...and let them have dominion over the fish of
the sea...
```

Of course, this means nothing unless we define the class epigraph, either in a STYLE tag or in a separate style sheet. An epigraph is a short verse or saying that appears at the beginning of a chapter or article.

```
epigraph
    {
    font-style: italic;
    font-weight: bold;
    text-align: center;
    }
```

Note that the definition of a class always begins with a period. Figure 18-3 shows the page, with the epigraph appearing centered and in bold italic type.

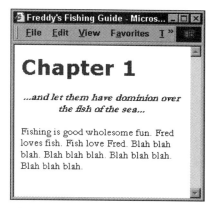

Figure 18-3
Centering and bold italic type set off this epigraph at the beginning of a chapter of text.

A complex Web site may use many different styles of text. Defining a class for each text style can save a tremendous amount of work, compared to applying styling to text elements individually. Of course, what kind of styling you choose to apply to a particular text element depends on the intended purpose of that element.

For example, consider a financial site that publishes analysts' opinions of the stock of various companies. For this kind of information to be useful, it's critical for the reader to know when the information was written. The publisher of our example site decides that every article on the site must list the date when the article was last updated, directly below the heading of the article. To further call attention to this important information, the publisher wants it to appear in red, and in bold type. In the site's style sheet, we create a class called updated as follows:

```
updated
   {
   color: red;
   font-weight: bold;
   }
```

In every article on the site, the date of the last revision appears directly below the heading. This date is styled according to the updated class, and thus appears in bold red type, as in Listing 18-4.

Listing 18-4:

```
<H1>Fish Incorporated - Analyst's Report</H1>

<P CLASS="updated">Updated June 13, 2001</P>

<P>This stock is overvalued. The company's last earnings report
was disappointing, and we don't recommend that you buy it right
now.</P>
```

To illustrate how easy it is to make site-wide changes to a site that uses CSS, let's say that the publisher decides that the dates in the preceding example are still not eye-catching enough. Because the style sheet doesn't specify a type size for the updated class, text using this class appears at the browser's default size. To make the updated class use 16-point type (fairly large), simply add this line to the definition of the updated class in the site's style sheet:

```
font-size: 16pt;
```

Once this change is made, all text belonging to the updated class appears in 16-point type, even though there may be hundreds of pages on the site that use this class.

In Session 6, you learn to set type size as a number from 1 to 7 by using the FONT tag. When using CSS, however, you set font sizes in *points* (abbreviated as pt). Points are a standard measurement in the printing world.

Done!

REVIEW

In this session, you have learned more about using style sheets:

- Making sure style sheets work as desired
- Creating special formatting by using inline styles
- Defining your own classes for custom styling

QUIZ YOURSELF

---

1. If you want a rule to apply to all text elements, what selector should you use for the rule? (See "Creating Trouble-free Style Sheets.")

2. How can you include several selectors in one rule? (See "Creating Trouble-free Style Sheets.")

3. An element can be affected by more than one style sheet. When two such style sheets conflict, which one will take precedence? (See "Using Inline Styles.")

4. What HTML tags can take the CLASS attribute? (See "Creating Custom Styles.")

5. Where do you define a class? (See "Creating Custom Styles.")

Using CSS for Positioning: the DIV Tag

Session Checklist

✔ Creating divisions by using the DIV tag

✔ Using a positioning class for consistent page layout

✔ Creating overlapping layers

Cascading Style Sheets (CSS) is far more than a tool for formatting text. It can also be used as a positioning tool that's even more powerful than tables. CSS enables you to specify the exact location for any element on a Web page.

30 Min.
To Go

Introducing the DIV Tag

The DIV (Division) tag is a very handy tool that was introduced with HTML 4.0. Its concept is simple: it enables you to define a group of elements as a division. Its power is great; once you define a division, you can control its format and positioning in ways that no other tag lets you do.

The DIV tag can be used to align text by using the optional ALIGN attribute, as in Listing 19-1:

Listing 19-1:

```
<DIV ALIGN="center">
This division is centered.
</DIV>

<P>
<DIV ALIGN="right">
This division is right-aligned.
</DIV>

<P>
<DIV ALIGN="justify">
You can even justify text with divisions. Although, to be fair,
you can do the same thing with the ALIGN attribute of the
Paragraph tag.
</DIV>
```

Figure 19-1 shows how the various types of text alignment look on a Web page.

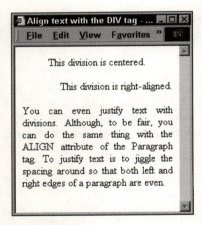

Figure 19-1
Various text-alignment effects achieved using the ALIGN attribute of the DIV tag

You can align text by using the ALIGN attribute of the P tag. In either case, the "justify" option doesn't work on older legacy browsers. To *justify* text is to use variable spacing so that both the left and right edges of a paragraph are straight and even.

The real power of the DIV tag, however, is revealed when you use it in conjunction with CSS. You can manipulate over 50 possible properties of an element by using CSS. Because the DIV tag imposes no formatting of its own (unless you use the optional ALIGN attribute), you can use it to enclose any group of elements in a *box* and can apply whatever styles you like to the box as a whole.

You can use CSS positioning properties to place such a box or division anywhere on a page. In Session 12, you use tables to create a sidebar. You can achieve the same effect by using two sets of DIV tags, as shown in Listing 19-2:

Listing 19-2:

```
<BODY>

<DIV
STYLE="
position: absolute;
width: 130;
top: 20px;
left: 20px;
padding: 6px;
background-color: #00FFFF;
">
Here is a nice little sidebar.
</DIV>

<DIV
STYLE="
position: absolute;
top: 20px;
left: 180px;
padding: 6px;
">
This is the main column.
</DIV>

</BODY>
```

Figure 19-2 shows the resulting page.

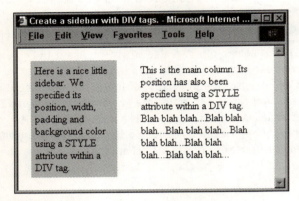

Figure 19-2
A left sidebar and right main column created by using DIV tags

You learn to create a sidebar by using tables in Session 12.

Positioning elements by using divisions is conceptually similar to positioning them by using table cells, although the code syntax is quite different. As with tables, you can specify sizes in either absolute (pixel) or relative (percentage) values, and you can specify padding, background colors, and much more. In this example, we've chosen absolute positioning and have specified the size and location of the two boxes in pixels. The first box appears 20 pixels from the top of the screen and 20 pixels from the left edge; it is 130 pixels wide. The second box is positioned 180 pixels from the left edge, so it appears 30 pixels to the right of the first box (20 + 130 + 30 = 180).

Unlike tables, divisions don't force you to think in terms of rows and columns. A division can be any size and can be placed anywhere on a page. Also, as you learn later in this session, a division can control text formatting. Refer to a good HTML/CSS reference to get even more ideas for wonderful things you can do to control the layout of your Web pages.

**20 Min.
To Go**

Defining a Positioning Class

In the previous example, you have created two divisions, each of which has defined its own styling and positioning. However, just as most Web sites have a consistent set of fonts and text styles, most sites have some standard page layouts that their pages all adhere to. In Session 18, you learn to define a class and to invoke the styling of that class from any HTML tag. If you create a class that specifies a certain positioning, you can use that positioning for any element simply by including it in a DIV tag with the appropriate CLASS attribute.

For example, create a class called sidebar by adding the following code to your site's style sheet:

```
.sidebar {
position: absolute;
width: 130;
height: 100%;
top: 20px;
left: 20px;
padding: 6px;

font-family: Verdana, Arial, Helvetica,
font-size: 12pt;
background-color: #00FFFF;
}
```

Here we've defined not only the position, but a background color and a font. Any HTML element with CLASS="sidebar" shares these characteristics. For example:

```
<DIV CLASS="sidebar">
Sidebar text
</DIV>
```

This creates a sidebar in the position defined in the sidebar class. Of course, a sidebar without a main column is no more useful than a hat without a head, so add the following code to your style sheet to create a class for the main section of the page, which we'll call maincol:

```
.maincol {
position: absolute;
top: 20px;
left: 180px;
padding: 6px;

font-family: times;
font-size: 12pt;
color: black;
}
```

Now that you've defined the sidebar and maincol classes, you can use the following HTML code (Listing 19-3) to create a typical two-column page:

Listing 19-3:

```
<HEAD>
     <LINK REL="stylesheet" HREF="style_sheet_two.css">
</HEAD>

<BODY>

<DIV CLASS="sidebar">
Sidebar content
</DIV>

<DIV CLASS="maincol">
Main column content
</DIV>

</BODY>
```

Note that the LINK element creates a link to the style sheet called style_sheet_two.css. This style sheet contains the definitions of the sidebar and maincol classes. Figure 19-3 shows this layout applied to a page from our fictional Freddy's Fishing Guide site.

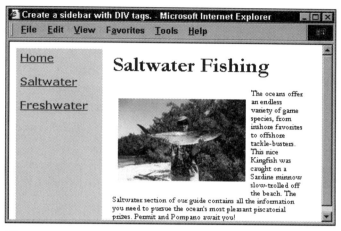

Figure 19-3
A page from Freddy's Fishing Guide, redesigned by using style sheets. This is the same basic page layout we create in Session 12, but we accomplish this layout by using divisions instead of tables. Each of two DIV elements refers to a CLASS, which defines positioning, text styling, and background color.

How concise and efficient this is compared with doing the same thing with tables! This efficiency, as well as greater precision and a larger range of properties that can be manipulated, makes CSS a superior tool for most formatting tasks. I recommend you use it whenever practical.

CSS doesn't work with older browsers (previous to 4.0 or so). If reaching users who have legacy browsers is important, you have to forgo the finer points of CSS or create alternate non-CSS pages for your browser-challenged visitors.

**10 Min.
To Go**

Creating Overlapping Layers

Next you'll learn a positioning trick that's impossible using tables: making layers of text or images overlap one another. When we define the sidebar and maincol classes that we use in Listing 19-3, we have to be careful to position the right-hand division far enough to the right to clear the left-hand division (plus a bit of a margin). If we don't, the two overlap.

The key to controlling overlapping layers is the `z-index` property. This property lets you specify a vertical stacking order for elements. The higher the z-index, the higher it appears in the stacking order. In Listing 19-4, the first division has a z-index of 2, and the second division has a z-index of 1. Thus, the first division appears on top (Figure 19-4).

Listing 19-4:

```
<DIV STYLE="
position: absolute;
width: 130;
height: 130;
top: 20px;
left: 20px;

z-index: 2;

background-color: #00FFFF;
">
Top Layer.
</DIV>

<DIV STYLE="
position: absolute;
width: 130;
height: 130;
top: 60px;
left: 60px;

z-index: 1;

background-color: #00cccc;
">
Bottom Layer. Bottom Layer. Bottom Layer. Bottom Layer.
<BR><BR>
 Bottom Layer.
</DIV>
```

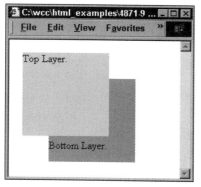

Figure 19-4
Two divisions with overlapping position properties. The one with the higher z-index appears on top.

Let's spruce up Freddy's home page by making the graphic heading float over the left-hand column. To do this, we need to create one more class in the style sheet; we'll call this the floating_head class:

```
.floating_head {
position:    absolute;
top:         0px;
left:        20px;
padding:     6px;
visibility:  visible;
z-index:     2;
}
```

Open the file from Listing 19-3, and add a division that contains Freddy's logo. Make this division a member of the floating_head class:

```
<DIV CLASS="floating_head">
<IMG SRC="images/freds_logo.gif" HEIGHT="60" WIDTH="468"
ALT="Freddy's Fishing Guide Logo">
</DIV>
```

In this example, it doesn't matter where you place this division in the code. However, if the z-index is *not specified*, divisions are stacked according to the order in which they appear in the code. Figure 19-5 shows Freddy's redesigned home page.

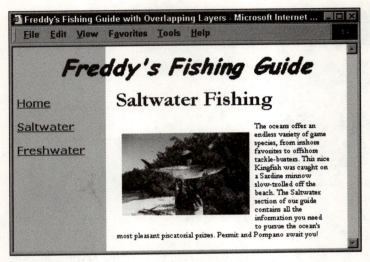

Figure 19-5
Freddy's home page now sports a light-blue left sidebar. The graphic heading floats over the sidebar and the main column.

Done!

REVIEW

In this session, you have learned to use the DIV tag in conjunction with CSS to position elements on a page. This has included:

- Using the DIV tag with inline styles
- Creating classes that define positioning
- Placing elements in overlapping layers

QUIZ YOURSELF

1. What sort of content can be between a pair of DIV tags? (See "Introducing the DIV Tag.")
2. What two CSS rules are required to create a division indented 40 pixels from the left side of a page? (See "Introducing the DIV Tag.")

3. If you create a class called sidebar, what code is required to create a division styled according to the sidebar class? (See "Defining a Positioning Class.")

4. What property allows you to specify the order of overlapping layers? (See "Creating Overlapping Layers.")

5. If that property is *not* specified, in what order are layers stacked? (See "Creating Overlapping Layers.")

20

Designing a Functional Web Site

✔ The components of a typical Web site

✔ Site structure and directory structure

✔ Creating a logical and consistent navigational scheme

**30 Min.
To Go**

Y ou've created several kinds of Web pages, but how these pages fit together into a complete Web site is something we haven't considered. A typical site has various kinds of pages to serve various functions, all of which should fit together into a whole that is effective and easy to use.

Sections of a Typical Web Site

Different site goals demand different ways of organizing content. But there are certain elements, or sections, that almost every site should have. A typical site has most, but not necessarily all, of the following sections:

- *Home page*. This is your front door, so make it attractive and well organized. The home page should make clear at a glance what's available on a site, but don't let it become cluttered. If there are too many links, consider grouping them on hub pages instead.

- *Main content hubs.* These pages group related content in whatever way is most logical for a particular site. A business site might have a hub for each main product category or for each of the markets the business serves. For example, a company that sells two main products might have a hub page for each product, or they might have a hub page for corporate customers and another for individuals. A hub page may contain a certain amount of content, but its main function is to provide links to pages with more specific information.

- *About the site owner.* It's critical for site users to know who stands behind the material on a site. For a business site, this section should contain a short history of the business; an educational site might focus on the authors' credentials. The main purpose of this section is to convince users that the site owner is reputable and trustworthy.

- *Contact details.* Every business site should provide full contact details, including the company's official street address and appropriate phone numbers. Freddy has no mailing address or phone, because he isn't real, and he can get by with only a feedback form. For a business site, however, this isn't acceptable. Nothing chases customers away faster than a site that makes it hard for users to contact the company. If you aren't selling anything you needn't be quite so careful about providing full contact details, but every site should list an e-mail contact at the very least. A site with no contact information is like an anonymous letter — people tend not to take it seriously.

- *Site map.* More complex sites may choose to offer a site map as a navigational aid for users. A site map is a graphical representation of a site's structure, similar to the representation in Figure 20-1.

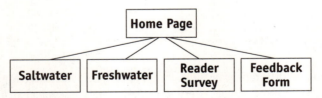

Figure 20-1
A site map or diagram showing the simple two-level site structure of Freddy's Fishing Guide

- *Search feature.* A good onsite search engine can add greatly to the usefulness of a site by enabling visitors to find information quickly about a particular topic. Most hosting services make some sort of search script available for you to incorporate into your site.

Appendix C on the CD-ROM lists some Web sites where you can find free scripts you can use to create an onsite search engine.

- *Links page.* Many sites feature links to related sites. For example, a future update to Freddy's site might add a list of other fishing-related Web resources. Trading reciprocal links with other sites is a good way to build traffic. To avoid cluttering pages with links, many sites choose to group all offsite links on a links page, often called "Web Resources," "Further Reading," or something similar.

Organizing a Web Site

A well-designed site has a consistent and logical *site structure*. The site structure is the way the site is organized from the user's perspective, determined by the way the pages are linked together. Freddy's site has a very simple structure with only two levels: the home page (top level) and the Freshwater and Saltwater hubs (second level), plus the reader survey and feedback forms.

You create the reader survey and the feedback forms in Session 16.

Figure 20-1 shows the structure of Freddy's site. More complex sites may have three, four or even more levels.

Site structure is not necessarily the same as *directory* structure, which refers to the way the files are organized on the Web server. For Freddy's site, we've placed all the HTML files in the same directory. Thus, the `saltwater.html` and `freshwater.html` files are *below* the `index.html` file in the site structure, but they all reside *at the same level* in the directory structure. Figure 20-2 shows the directory structure of Freddy's site, which is different from the site structure shown in Figure 20-1.

```
freds_fishing_guide
    index.html
    saltwater.html
    freshwater.html
    survey.html
    feedback.html
    images
        freds_logo.gif
        kingfish.jpg
        pargo.jpg
        tarpon.jpg
        etc.
```

Figure 20-2
For convenience, Freddy's HTML files reside in the same directory, but image files are grouped in their own subdirectory.

About file addressing

**20 Min.
To Go**

In Session 7, you learn two ways to reference a file in an HTML element. To create a link to the file `kingfish.jpg`, which lives in the `freds_fishing_guide/images` directory, you can use either *absolute file addressing*:

```
<IMG
SRC="http://www.freddysfishingguide.com/freds_fishing_guide/images
/kingfish.jpg">
```

or *default file addressing*:

```
<IMG SRC="images/kingfish.jpg">
```

This default link works *only* if the `images` directory is located in the same directory as the file containing the link. To link to files elsewhere in the directory structure, you need to learn two more methods of file addressing: *relative addressing* and *root addressing* (of course, absolute file addressing, which specifies the complete URL of a Web page, will always work, but shouldn't be used to link to pages within a site because it unnecessarily complicates the code and causes a slightly longer load time).

As Freddy has learned more Web design techniques, he's added features to his Fishing Guide site. However, he's decided to keep the original, basic version of the site alongside the new and improved version.

The `freds_fishing_guide` directory contains a simple version of the site, incorporating the techniques learned in the first few chapters. The `freds_fishing_guide_advanced` directory contains a more complex version of the site, with frames, style sheets and other advanced features.

This presents a problem, however. Both versions use the same images, which reside in the `freds_fishing_guide/images` directory. When we create the new version of the site, we must change all the hyperlinks that refer to images. If we don't, they won't work because the HTML files that point to them are now in a different directory.

Of course, we can create a duplicate `images` subdirectory under `freds_fishing_guide_advanced`, but that is a waste of hard disk space on the Web server, especially as image files tend to be large. Instead, link to the files in the `freds_fishing_guide/images` directory by using relative addressing:

```
<IMG SRC="../freds_fishing_guide/images/kingfish.jpg">
```

The double dots (`..`) indicate a movement up one level in the directory structure. Go up multiple levels by using multiple pairs of dots, for example:

```
<A HREF="../../../directory/file.html">
```

This relative link tells the user's browser to go up three levels in the directory structure, then to go to the directory called `directory` to find the file called `file.html`. Relative addressing can get complicated because every hyperlink must specify the exact path from the source file to the destination file. The fourth addressing method, root addressing, is simpler: an initial slash represents the root directory, and the file path is specified from the root, for example:

```
<IMG SRC="/freds_fishing_guide/images/kingfish.jpg">
```

This link works from any file in any directory under the root directory.

The concept of a Web site's root directory is discussed in Session 3.

The drawback to root addressing is that it works only on the Web server, not on your local machine (because the root directory isn't the same). So if you use root addressing, you can't test your hyperlinks until the pages are live on the server.

Creating a good navigational scheme

A typical Web site has a tree-like structure, with the home page as the root and the various sections branching off. You can also visualize a pyramid, with the

**10 Min.
To Go**

home page at the top corner. Keep this pyramid fairly close to an equal-sided triangle. Offering too many parallel links from the home page (site structure "too flat") is confusing: instead, group related pages together under a few hub pages. On the other hand, a structure that is "too tall" makes users click through several pages to get to the information they're looking for; avoid too-tall structures.

Figures 20-3, 20-4, and 20-5 show three hypothetical site structures.

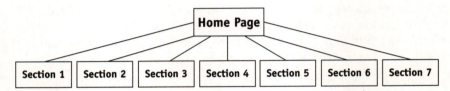

Figure 20-3
This site structure is too flat. The site would be easier to navigate if related pages were grouped under three or four hub pages, each linked from the home page.

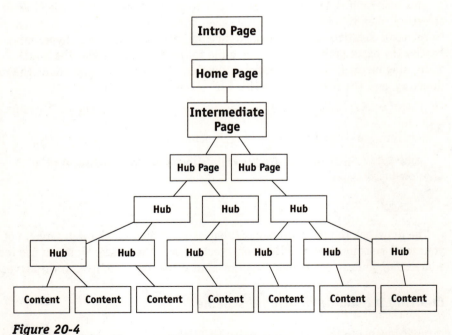

Figure 20-4
This site structure is too tall, forcing users to click through several unnecessary levels to get to the good stuff.

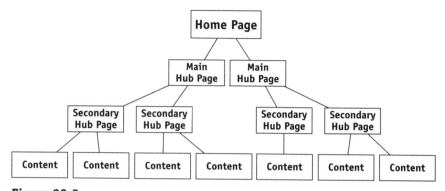

Figure 20-5
This site structure is just right, approximating an equal-sided triangle.

Follow these additional sound principles to create a navigational scheme that makes your site a pleasure to use:

- *Put content on every page.* Don't make your users click through page after page to find what they want. Remember that every page takes time to load and that Web surfers have very short attention spans.

- *Put your main content up front.* Whatever the main attraction of your site, feature it prominently on the home page and/or second-level hub pages; don't bury it. If your site is selling something, be sure the ordering page is *very* easy to find.

- *Use a consistent Navbar.* Users should be able to get to your home page and other main sections instantly from any page on your site.

- *Clearly label all links.* Let your users know exactly what happens when they click a link. Warn them if they're about to load a huge graphic or other slow-loading file.

Done!

REVIEW

In this session, you have learned some principles of good overall site design:

- Understanding sections of a typical site
- Organizing a Web site
- Creating a sound navigational scheme

QUIZ YOURSELF

1. What is a site map? (See "Sections of a Typical Web Site.")

2. What is a links page? (See "Sections of a Typical Web Site.")

3. What is the relationship between site structure and directory structure? (See "Organizing a Web Site.")

4. How do you create a link from a source file to a destination file if the two files are in parallel directories (at the same level in the directory structure)? (See "About File Addressing.")

5. What shape should a diagram of a well-designed site structure have? (See "Creating a Good Navigational Scheme.")

PART

IV

Saturday Evening

1. A Cascading Style Sheet (CSS) consists of rules. What does a rule consist of?

2. What does a CSS declaration consist of?

3. If a particular property is not mentioned in a style sheet, what determines how that property is displayed?

4. Name three ways in which you can apply a style sheet to a document.

5. If you want to apply a style sheet called `styles.css` to a group of HTML documents, what code must appear in each of those documents?

6. If you want to create a rule that applies to all text elements, what selector should you use?

7. Can you create a rule that has more than one selector?

8. How do you create an inline style?

9. If an element is affected by two style sheets and the style sheets conflict, which one style sheet takes precedence?

10. How can you create your own custom styles?

11. Once you've defined a class, what HTML elements can it apply to?

12. What type of content can you include in a `DIV` element?

13. If you want to create a division that begins 200 pixels from the top of a page, what two CSS rules are required?

14. What HTML code do you use to create a division that is styled according to a class named `leftcolumn`?

15. What property do you use to specify the order of overlapping layers?

16. What contact information should be included on every business Web site?

17. What are four types of file addressing?

18. How does site structure relate to directory structure?

19. What file address do you use to create a hyperlink *from* a source file that has the file path root/dir_one/file.html *to* a destination file that has the file path root/dir_two/file.html?

20. Name at least two sound principles for creating an effective navigational scheme.

☑ Friday

☑ Saturday

☑ Sunday

PART

V

Sunday Morning

SESSION

21

Creating Animations

Session Checklist

✔ Creating an animated .gif

✔ Using Flash animations

✔ About plug-ins

**30 Min.
To Go**

A little motion can add a lot of eye appeal to a Web page. But animated graphics are not only entertaining. They can be functional, too, as they enable you to deliver more information in the same amount of screen space. The animated .gif format makes it easy to create simple or complex animations.

Building an Animated .gif

In Session 10, you learn about two handy Web-specific features of the .gif graphic format: transparency and interlacing. Now you'll learn to use an even more exciting feature. A series of images can be grouped together as *frames* in an *animation* and stored in a single .gif file.

An animated .gif is made up of individual images, each of which is called a frame (no relation to HTML frames, discussed in Sessions 13 and 14). To create an animation, you must create the individual images, then assemble them using a program that can save animated `.gifs`. Most full-featured graphics packages can do this either natively or through a companion application, and several dedicated animation programs are also available, including GIF Construction Set Professional 2.0a (`http://www.mindworkshop.com/alchemy/gifcon.html`), Ulead GIF Animator 4.0 (`http://www.webutilities.com/products/GAni/runme.htm`), and GIFmation (`http://www.boxtopsoft.com/gifmation.html`).

A trial version of Paint Shop Pro is provided on this book's CD-ROM.

Create a simple, animated banner using Jasc Paint Shop Pro and its companion program, Animation Shop, by following these steps. If you're using a different animation package, the exact commands differ, but the basic process is the same.

1. Launch Paint Shop Pro, and create a new file 468-pixels wide and 60-pixels tall. This is a standard size for ad banners.

2. We'll assemble this banner from a couple of existing pieces of clip-art and some text. Open `html_examples/swordfish.tif`, as shown in Figure 21-1. Of course, you can also use any appropriately-sized image. Using the rectangle selection tool, select the entire image, and choose Ctrl+C to copy it to the clipboard.

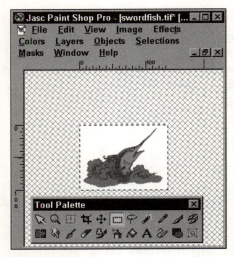

Figure 21-1
Copying a piece of clip-art from the CD-ROM to use in your banner

3. Now return to the window with your new file, and choose Edit ➪ Paste ➪ As New Selection. Place the swordfish at the left end of the canvas, as in Figure 21-2.

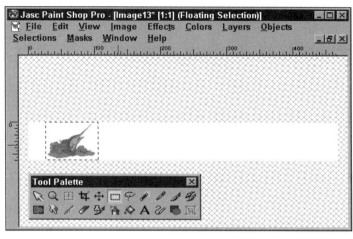

Figure 21-2
Pasting the image into the new file

4. Choose the Text tool, and place a large text headline to the right of the picture. Freddy asks the piscine question "Are billfish your bag?" in Web-safe dark blue (HTML color #000099) with a Comic Sans font. Figure 21-3 shows the completed image.

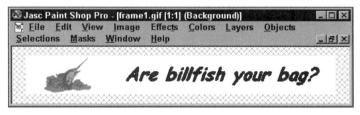

Figure 21-3
No artistic talent required! Assembling a banner from text and existing images.

5. Save this file as `frame1.gif`. This is the first frame of the animation. Save as a non-transparent `.gif` file.

6. Create another new 468×60 file, and open `trout.tif`. Copy and paste this image into your new file as you do with the swordfish, but this time put the fish on the right side of the banner.

7. Use the Text tool to place a headline to the left of the trout.

8. Figure 21-4 shows the result. Save this file as `frame2.gif`.

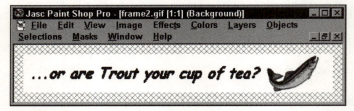

Figure 21-4
Second frame, pretty much the same

9. Repeat the preceding steps to create as many frames as you want.

10. Launch Animation Shop (File ⇨ Jasc Software Products ⇨ Launch Animation Shop) and start a new file. Specify a size of 468×60 and an Opaque (not Transparent) canvas.

**20 Min.
To Go**

If you are creating an image such as an ad banner that may be placed on someone else's Web site, don't make the image transparent; you never know what color background it may appear against.

11. Select Animation ⇨ Insert Frames ⇨ From File to load the individual frames you have created in the preceding steps. Figure 21-5 shows the Insert Frames dialog box. You can set the time between each frame in the "Delay time" box, in hundredths of a second. Set the delay time to "100" to create a pause of one second between frames.

12. Preview your animation in the Play window by choosing View ⇨ Animation. You can edit the animation in the Frames window. Figure 21-6 shows the Play and Frames windows. When you are satisfied, simply save the animation as a new `.gif` file.

13. Include this animation in a Web page just as you do any `.gif` file by using the `IMG` tag.

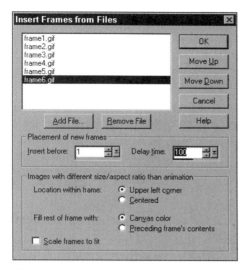

Figure 21-5
Adding frames to an animation by using the Insert Frames dialog box in Jasc Animation Shop

Figure 21-6
The upper Play window previews the animation, and you can edit it in the lower Frames window.

Using Flash Animations

The preceding example is only a small taste of what you can do with the animated .gif format. With a little imagination, you can create much more complex animations. However, an even more powerful tool for creating animations has become very popular among Web designers: Flash, from Macromedia.

Flash is a commercial software package that offers a complete animation studio. There isn't room here to explain how to use Flash to create animations. Instead, try the fine book *Flash 5 Weekend Crash Course*, also from Hungry Minds, Inc. The Flash authoring software package can produce a finished animation in several different formats, including the animated .gif format.

Flash offers a very sophisticated environment for creating animations, but it does have certain drawbacks compared to the simpler animated .gif format, as listed in Table 21-1:

Table 21-1
.gif Animations versus Flash Animations

Animated .gif Format	Macromedia Flash
Supported by most browsers with no plug-in required	Requires plug-in, which may be downloaded free
No audio support	Flash animations can include audio
Many authoring tools available, some of them free or low-cost shareware	Authoring requires Flash software package

About Plug-ins

Web browsers can recognize a variety of file types. As you know, they can display not only HTML files but also the graphic formats .gif, .jpg and .png. In addition to these *natively supported* file types, a Web browser can display a huge variety of other file types if the browser has the appropriate plug-in installed.

A *plug-in* is a software application that extends the capabilities of a Web browser by enabling it to recognize a certain file type or group of file types. Viewing any type of media a browser doesn't natively support requires a plug-in. Most plug-ins are free and are available for download. In addition to Macromedia's

Flash animations, discussed in the previous section, file formats that may require a plug-in include streaming audio/video formats such as RealMedia and QuickTime (discussed in Session 23).

When a user requests a file that requires a plug-in that is not installed, a dialog box pops up to inform the user of the particular plug-in required. More sophisticated sites even provide a direct link to a site where the plug-in can be downloaded. Once the user has downloaded and installed the appropriate plug-in, it is launched automatically any time a file of that type is encountered. For example, once the Flash plug-in is properly installed on your system, Flash animations on any Web site you visit should function properly with no additional input on your part.

Downloading and installing a plug-in is easy, but there are always certain Web users who don't go to the trouble, can't figure out how it works, or simply don't want to install a plug-in on their system. Therefore, you must assume that any time you use media that requires a plug-in, a certain percentage of users won't be able to experience it. As with other advanced features such as frames and CSS, if you want to reach as many potential users as possible, give users the option of choosing alternative pages that get your message across without requiring plug-ins.

You learn more about plug-ins in the upcoming session on Web audio and video.

Done!

REVIEW

In this session, you have learned to enable Web page users to send feedback. This has included:

- Building an animated `.gif` using clip-art and text
- Using Flash animations versus animated `.gifs`
- Using browser plug-ins

QUIZ YOURSELF

1. What file extension does a `.gif` animation use? (See "Building an Animated `.gif`.")

2. What are the component parts of an animated `.gif`? (See "Building an Animated `.gif`.")

3. Why shouldn't an ad banner use the transparent `.gif` format? (See "Building an Animated `.gif`.")

4. Name two differences between a `.gif` animation and a Flash animation. (See "Using Flash Animations.")

5. What happens if a user visits a page containing a Flash animation, but the user's browser does not have the Flash plug-in installed? (See "About Plug-ins.")

Building a Graphic Navbar

Session Checklist

✔ Creating graphic navigational elements

✔ Building a navbar from individual buttons

✔ Using image maps

In previous sessions, you create a text navbar for Freddy's Fishing Guide. This navbar includes links to all main sections of the site. In this session, you'll make Freddy's navbar more distinctive and a little more eye-catching by replacing the text links with graphic elements.

**30 Min.
To Go**

Creating Navigational Buttons

You can create a button for each section of Freddy's site by using the same techniques you use to create a banner in Session 21.

What's the difference between a banner and a button? Basically, size. A banner is a fairly wide graphic element, for example, a page heading. The advertising community has established 468×60 pixels as a standard size for ad banners. A button is a smaller graphic element, of an appropriate size to include in a sidebar, or a top or bottom bar.

1. Launch your graphic editor, and start a new file. This time, make the size 120-pixels wide by 24-pixels high.

2. Using the Text tool, add the word "Home" in Freddy's house style (Comic Sans font, dark blue), as shown in Figure 22-1.

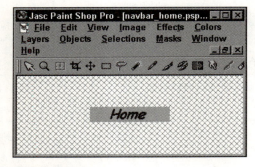

Figure 22-1
Creating a graphic-text navbar button in Paint Shop Pro

3. Save the file in your graphic editor's native file format (for Paint Shop Pro, it's `.psp`). Use this as the master file for all future modifications.

4. Now save the file as `navbar_home.gif`. Be sure that you're saving in the `.gif` format and that the transparency option is selected. This is the finished navbar button.

`.gifs` and `.jpgs` are compressed files, intended as end-user formats only. Although it's possible to open and edit a `.gif` file, this can yield unpredictable results. For any file that you might want to edit later, save a version in your graphic editor's native format or as a `.tif` or `.bmp` file.

5. Return to the master file, and change the text to "Saltwater."

6. Save this as `navbar_salt.gif`.

7. Repeat the preceding steps until you have as many buttons as you want.

Now assemble these buttons into a complete navbar. In Session 19, you create a sidebar division by using the DIV tag. Place IMG links to your new buttons within this sidebar division, and make each button a hyperlink to the appropriate section, as shown in Listing 22-1:

**20 Min.
To Go**

You learn to make an image a hyperlink in Session 8.

Listing 22-1:

```
<DIV CLASS="sidebar">

<BR><BR><BR><BR>

<A HREF="index.html"><IMG
SRC="../freds_fishing_guide/images/navbar_home.gif" WIDTH="120"
HEIGHT="24" BORDER="0" ALT="Return to the Home Page"></A>
<BR>

<A HREF="saltwater.html"><IMG
SRC="../freds_fishing_guide/images/navbar_salt.gif" WIDTH="120"
HEIGHT="24" BORDER="0" ALT="Saltwater Fishing"></A>
<BR>

<A HREF="freshwater.html"><IMG
SRC="../freds_fishing_guide/images/navbar_fresh.gif" WIDTH="120"
HEIGHT="24" BORDER="0" ALT="Freshwater Fishing"></A>
<BR>

<A HREF="survey.html"><IMG
SRC="../freds_fishing_guide/images/navbar_survey.gif" WIDTH="120"
HEIGHT="24" BORDER="0" ALT="Take our reader survey">
</A>
<BR>

<A HREF="feedback.html"><IMG
SRC="../freds_fishing_guide/images/navbar_feedback.gif"
WIDTH="120" HEIGHT="24" BORDER="0" ALT="Send email to Freddy"></A>

</DIV>
```

Note that we've placed a Break (BR) tag between images to space them out a little. Figure 22-2 shows the resulting page. If you have trouble getting your images to line up just right, you can force them into position using a table or a set of divisions.

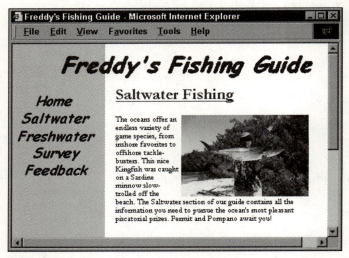

Figure 22-2
The navbar at the left consists of five graphic images, each linked to the appropriate page of Freddy's site.

Creating an Image Map

In the preceding example, we create five buttons and make each a hyperlink. However, it's possible to create a navbar from a single image, defining different areas of the image as hyperlinks with different destinations. You can do this by means of an *image map*.

Of course, image maps are not just for navbars. Any time you want to have an image with clickable *hot spots*, use an image map. However, to continue the navbar example, let's say that Freddy wants to include a background image in his navbar. Whether you think this shows good taste or not, it does happen to be a job for an image map.

To build a navbar that uses an image map, create an image similar to navbar2.jpg, which is shown in Figure 22-3:

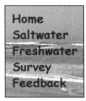

Figure 22-3
Freddy's new and (perhaps) improved navbar, consisting of a single graphic image.

1. Launch your graphic editor, and start a new file 120-pixels wide and 144-pixels high.

2. Find a suitable background image, and size it so that it's also 120×144.

3. Copy the background image, and paste it into your new file.

4. A background image should be very light so it doesn't obscure the foreground elements. If needed, increase the brightness and/or decrease the contrast of the image until it is very light and discreet, as shown in Figure 22-4 (In Paint Shop Pro, choose Colors ⇨ Adjust ⇨ Brightness ⇨ Contrast).

Figure 22-4
Lightening up an image in Paint Shop Pro's Brightness/Contrast dialog box

5. Use the Text tool to add the titles of the Web-site sections to the file, as in the previous example. This time, however, arrange all of these titles within this single image.

6. When the image looks as you want it to, save it as a native-format master file and again as `navbar2.jpg`.

7. Insert the image into a Web page by using the following code. We're placing it in our pre-defined sidebar division, as in the previous example; of course, you can place the image and its accompanying map anywhere on the page.

```
<DIV CLASS="sidebar">

<BR><BR><BR><BR>

<MAP NAME="navbar">
<AREA COORDS="0,0,120,34" HREF="index.html" >
<AREA COORDS="0,35,120,60" HREF="saltwater.html" >
<AREA COORDS="0,61,120,86" HREF="freshwater.html" >
<AREA COORDS="0,87,120,110" HREF="survey.html" >
<AREA COORDS="0,111,120,144" HREF="feedback.html" >
</MAP>

<IMG SRC="../freds_fishing_guide/images/navbar2.jpg" WIDTH="120"
HEIGHT="144" BORDER="0" ALT="Fred's Navbar" USEMAP="#navbar">

</DIV>
```

Note that the image is *not* linked using an Anchor tag. Instead, the IMG tag contains the USEMAP attribute, which refers to a map that we've named navbar. The map is defined by a MAP element, which can contain any number of AREA tags. Each AREA tag defines a hot spot by using the COORDS attribute and links the hot spot to a destination file by using the HREF attribute. The size and shape of each rectangular hot spot is defined using two pairs of *x and y coordinates*. An x coordinate specifies a horizontal distance in pixels from the left edge of the image, and a y coordinate specifies a vertical distance in pixels from the top of the image. The first pair of coordinates specifies the location of the top-left corner of the rectangle, and the second pair specifies the location of the bottom-right corner.

For example:

```
COORDS="0,0,120,144"
```

This creates a hot spot covering the entire image because the size of the image is 120×144. By defining five AREAs with appropriate x and y coordinates, we've created five hot spots that line up with the locations of the five section titles.

In this example, the image is divided vertically into hot spots, but they can also be horizontal (that is, side by side). Hot spots can overlap, but there's no point in overlapping them; you want each hot spot to point to a particular destination.

Figure 22-5 shows Freddy's home page with the new navbar.

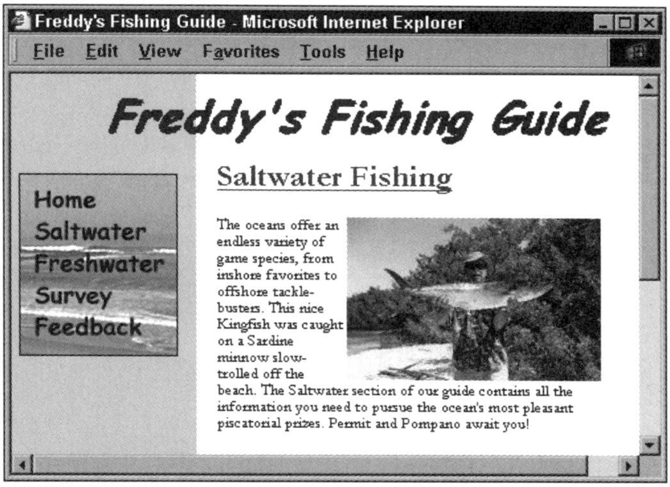

Figure 22-5
The new navbar uses an image map to link rectangular hot spots to the appropriate Web pages.

Note

Should you use graphic text or HTML text for things such as headings and navbars? Graphic text enables you to use whatever font you like and to combine text and pictures as you do in the second part of this session. However, graphic text takes longer to load and is more difficult to modify than HTML text.

To get your hot spots to line up just the way you want them, you must figure out the right values for the COORDS attribute, which can be a very tedious process. Several software applications automate the process for you, enabling you to create image maps by using a graphical interface. Web Hotspots v4.02 and Mapedit 3.2 are two such image map editors. Both these handy utilities are shareware.

CD-ROM

Web Hotspots v4.02 and Mapedit 3.2 are included on this book's accompanying CD-ROM. Appendix C on the CD-ROM lists several sites where you can find other shareware applications.

Done!

REVIEW

In this session, you have learned to create a navbar by using graphic elements instead of text. This has included:

- Creating navigational buttons
- Assembling several buttons into a navbar
- Creating clickable hot spots in a graphic by using an image map

QUIZ YOURSELF

1. When you create a graphic navbar button, you save it in your graphic editor's native format before saving it as a .gif or .jpg. Why? (See "Creating Navigational Buttons.")
2. How can you assemble individual buttons into a complete navbar? (See "Creating Navigational Buttons.")
3. What is a hot spot? (See "Creating an Image Map.")
4. What two elements are used to define an image map? (See "Creating an Image Map.")
5. A rectangular hot spot is defined by four numbers. What do these numbers mean? (See "Creating an Image Map.")

Audio and Video for the Web

Session Checklist

✔ Understanding digital audio and video basics

✔ Minimizing load time for audio and video files

✔ Understanding the various Web audio and video formats

**30 Min.
To Go**

The Web is by no means limited to text and graphics. As Internet bandwidth increases, audio, video, and other types of media are becoming more common on the Web. Multimedia continues to present its own set of challenges, however, so you need to learn the basics of digital audio and video before you can add these media effectively to your Web site.

Minimizing Download Times

In Session 7, you learn that graphic files are much larger than text files and must be handled with care to avoid excessive page-load times. Well, audio files are much bigger than graphic files, and video files are absolutely enormous. For example, a one-second clip of CD-quality audio has a file size of approximately 172 kilobytes;

one second of uncompressed video can have a file size of 30 megabytes! These media files are so large that it wouldn't be practical to use them at all if powerful techniques were not available to minimize their download times.

You've learned three ways to minimize the long download times associated with graphic files: keep their physical measurements small; reduce their resolution (at the cost of a trade-off in image quality); and use compressed file formats (`.gif`, `.jpg`, and `.png`). Putting audio and video on the Web involves the heavy use of all three of these techniques, as well as a fourth technique called streaming.

Audio file size

Three parameters affect the size of an audio file:

1. *Sample rate.* Digital audio is created by taking a series of *samples*, or digital "snapshots," of a sound. The higher the sample rate, the higher the quality of the audio. The audio on a compact disc (CD) has a sample rate of 44,100 samples per second.

2. *Bit resolution.* The digital audio recording process assigns a number to each sample, which is represented by a fixed number of bits. The higher the bit rate, the higher the audio quality. CD audio has a resolution of 16 bits.

3. *Number of channels.* An audio recording can be *mono* (one channel) or *stereo* (two channels). Stereo recordings sound a little more realistic because each ear hears a slightly different signal, as it does when you are listening to a live musical performance. Because it consists of two separate channels, a stereo audio file is twice the size of a mono audio file. Generally, stereo is used only for music, not for speech or other sounds.

The audio format used for compact discs, often referred to as *CD-quality audio*, is 44,100 samples per second, 16-bit stereo. This is a high-quality format, but it results in very large files: about 10 megabytes per minute of audio! This is much too large to be used on the Web, so the first thing you want to do when preparing audio clips for Web use is reduce the sample rate, bit resolution, number of channels, or all three.

Converting to mono halves file sizes with no actual loss of quality, so most Web audio is mono. Halving the bit resolution halves the file size but at the expense of a slight loss of quality. Reducing the sample rate involves the same trade-off. Note that different types of audio demand different levels of quality. Music requires a higher level of quality than voice does.

Usually, a format of 8 bits, 22,050 samples per second, mono is considered adequate for Web music and has a file size one eighth that of CD-quality audio. You can squeeze the file size even more by reducing the sample rate further, but if you go much below 11,025 samples per second, you'll probably find the quality level too low for music. Speech, however, is often rendered at 8,000 samples per second, and most people find it to be of adequate quality.

**20 Min.
To Go**

Video file size

Three factors affect the size of a video file:

1. *Screen size*. Obviously, an audio file has no physical measurements, but a video file does, which is why most Web video appears in tiny "postage stamp" windows.

2. *Resolution*. A video file, like a still image, has a resolution that can be expressed in pixels per inch. The higher the resolution, the larger the file size. You can set the resolution when preparing a video file for the Web. If the resolution is too low, the picture appears grainy or blocky.

3. *Frame Rate*. A movie creates the illusion of motion by displaying a series of still pictures (frames) at a fixed rate. Film uses a frame rate of 24 frames per second (fps), and VHS video uses approximately 30 fps. Reducing the frame rate reduces the file size but makes the motion less smooth and more "jerky." At frame rates below 15 fps, the illusion of continuous motion is lost.

Compression and streaming

There are many ways to compress audio and video files. A compression scheme or algorithm is known as a *codec* because it codes and decodes data. Usually, Web video is in the .mpeg format, which allows various codecs to be used. The most popular compressed audio format is MP3 (.mpeg Layer 3), which you learn about later in this session.

Streaming was invented in the early days of the Web as a way to get around long download times. Although most files must be fully downloaded before they can be played, a streaming file can begin playing before the entire file is downloaded. Streaming, which works with both audio and video, has two additional advantages: it enables continuous live broadcasting over the Web, and it allows users to listen to (or view) a file without allowing them to copy it to their hard drives.

**10 Min.
To Go**

Audio and Video Formats for the Web

Different formats are appropriate for different applications, as you learn in more detail in Session 24. Note that pretty much all these formats allow you to specify parameters such as bit resolution, sample rate, number of channels (for audio), frame rate (for video), and so on. For example, a .wav file can be 44,100 samples per second, 16-bit stereo, 11,025 samples per second 8-bit mono, or any other desired settings. Also, although some formats were originally associated with particular platforms, nowadays all major media players support all major formats. For example, there's no need to offer a file in separate Windows and Mac formats.

Audio formats may be categorized as *source* formats, *compressed* formats, and *streaming* formats. A source format is an uncompressed format that can be used either for high-quality source files or end-user Web files. Because their file sizes are large, source formats should be used as end-user Web files for very short audio clips only. Audio source formats include .wav (originally a Windows format), .aiff (originally a Mac format), .au, and .snd.

Among compressed audio formats, by far the most popular is .mp3. .mp3 uses an intelligent compression scheme that removes only those parts of the signal that are usually masked and unheard anyway, resulting in good audio quality at a very small file size. .mp3 is the preferred format for downloadable audio files.

Streaming audio formats include RealNetworks' RealMedia format (.ra and .ram file extensions) and Micorosoft's Windows Media Format (.wmf file extension).

MIDI

Musical Instrument Digital Interface (MIDI) is not an audio format. It's a code for sending instructions to an electronic musical instrument telling it how to perform a piece of music. The difference between an audio file and a MIDI file is a bit like the difference between a bitmap graphic file and a vector graphic file. In Session 9, you learn that a bitmap graphic file contains a pixel-by-pixel representation of an image, but a vector graphic file contains only a set of instructions for recreating that image. Likewise, an audio file consists of a digital recording of a sound, but a MIDI file consists of a set of instructions that an appropriate device (a synthesizer) can use to recreate a musical performance. MIDI files use a .mid file extension.

Most sound cards can play back both audio and MIDI files because they contain two separate devices: an audio recording/playback device and a synthesizer. A *synthesizer* is an electronic musical instrument that can produce a range of artificially generated sounds. How many sounds are available, and how realistic they sound, depends entirely on the synthesizer.

MIDI has attracted a lot of attention from Web developers because MIDI files are tiny compared to audio files. In my opinion, however, MIDI is not a suitable format for adding music to Web sites for three reasons:

1. There are many types of sound cards, and each has a different set of available sounds. The *General MIDI* specification standardizes this a bit by providing a standard set of program numbers that correspond to the most commonly-used musical sounds. However, not all sound cards conform to the General MIDI specification, and even those that do may sound very different from one another. If you use MIDI music on a Web site, it's very likely that the user will hear something completely different from what the composer has intended.

2. The synthesizers included on consumer sound cards are of very low quality, producing music that sounds "cheesy" even to the untutored ear.

3. MIDI is solely useful for instrumental music, as it cannot record voices, sound effects, or any other sounds.

Various Video formats

All video formats used on the Web use some form of compression. Video formats include .avi (originally a Windows format) and .mov (originally a Mac format). .mpeg is the most popular Web video format. Any of the streaming formats can also include video.

Done!

REVIEW

In this session, you have learned the basics of digital audio and video. This has included:

- Techniques for minimizing load time
- Basic concepts of file compression and streaming
- Characteristics of different audio and video formats

QUIZ YOURSELF

1. What are the three parameters that affect the size of an audio file? (See "Minimizing Download Times.")

2. What are the values of these parameters for "CD-quality" audio? (See "Minimizing Download Times.")

3. What is streaming? (See "Minimizing Download Times.")

4. What's the difference between a .wav file and an .mp3 file? (See "Audio and Video Formats for the Web.")

5. What's the most popular Web video format? (See "Audio and Video Formats for the Web.")

Adding Audio and Video to a Site

Session Checklist

✔ Adding audio or video to a Web site

✔ Understanding common Web-audio applications

✔ Using audio and video software

In Session 23, you learn that various audio and video formats are in use on the Web. Now you'll learn to include audio and video files in a Web page, as well as which formats are appropriate for which situations.

**30 Min.
To Go**

Including Audio or Video in a Web Page

You can make audio and video files available on a Web site in several different ways. The simplest way is to create a hyperlink to an audio or video file by using the trusty old A tag.

```
<A HREF="sounds/dog_bark.wav">Click to hear a dog bark</A>.
```

This element creates a link to a .wav audio file called dog_bark.wav. When the user clicks this link, one of two things happens depending on how the user's browser is configured:

1. A media player (plug-in) pops up and plays the sound file.
2. The browser prompts the user either to play the sound file or to download it and save it to the user's hard drive.

You can use the A tag to create a link to any type of file, including video.

```
<A HREF="clip_one.mov">Click to play video clip</A>.
```

This element creates a link to a video file in the .mov format.

 More recent browsers come with media player plug-ins installed. Older browsers require the user to download and install the necessary plug-in. To hear audio, the user's system must have a sound card, and the sound card must be hooked up to an amplifier and speakers.

The EMBED tag provides another way to present audio or video on a Web page. The EMBED tag causes an onscreen player to be displayed on the page. Optional attributes of the EMBED tag enable you to control the appearance of the player as well as several things about the way the sound is played.

Some possible attributes of the EMBED tag are:

*   HEIGHT and WIDTH. These control the size of the onscreen player. If HEIGHT and WIDTH are not specified, the entire media player appears on the Web page. (The type of player that appears on the Web page depends on the browser: the default media player for Internet Explorer is Windows Media Player.)
*   HIDDEN. If you specify HIDDEN="true", the player is invisible. This overrides any values set in the HEIGHT and WIDTH attributes.
*   AUTOSTART. If you specify AUTOSTART="true", the file automatically plays as soon as the page loads.

The EMBED tag can take some of the same attributes used with the IMG tag, such as ALIGN, ALT, and BORDER. You can make text wrap around the media player by using the ALIGN attribute. Listing 24-1 has three EMBED elements. The first element doesn't specify HEIGHT or WIDTH, so the player is displayed full size. The second element specifies a smaller size, so only the transport controls are displayed. The third element creates a tiny player.

Listing 24-1:

```
<EMBED SRC="../freds_fishing_guide_advanced/sounds/dog_bark.wav"
ALIGN="left">

<P>At left we have embedded the entire Windows Media Player.
However, we can also embed a smaller version, with just the
necessary transport controls shown, by setting HEIGHT and WIDTH
attributes in the EMBED tag.

<P>
<EMBED SRC="../freds_fishing_guide_advanced/sounds/dog_bark.wav"
WIDTH="140" HEIGHT="40" ALIGN="right">

As with images, you can make text wrap around a media player by
using the ALIGN, HSPACE and VSPACE attributes in the EMBED tag.
This text wraps around the player.

<EMBED SRC="../freds_fishing_guide_advanced/sounds/dog_bark.wav"
WIDTH="60" HEIGHT="20" ALIGN="left">

You can even make a tiny little player like the one at left. Just
don't make it too small to display the Play and Pause controls.
```

The resulting Web page is shown in Figure 24-1.

Like the A tag, you can use the EMBED tag with any type of file, including any audio or video format. Of course, whether or not the file can be played depends on the media player installed on a user's system, but current media players can handle all common audio and video formats.

You can add video to a Web page in the same way that you add audio, with one important difference. Like a static image file, but unlike an audio file, a video file has a set display size. In Session 23, you learn that a smaller display size means a smaller file size. This is why Web video is almost always presented in a small window, a fraction of the total size of the screen. If you specify HEIGHT and WIDTH attributes in an EMBED element, their values must be large enough to accommodate the display size of the video file, with enough space left over for the transport controls. The amount of space required for the transport controls depends on the user's browser and media player. Be sure to test any page that contains audio or video on a variety of user systems.

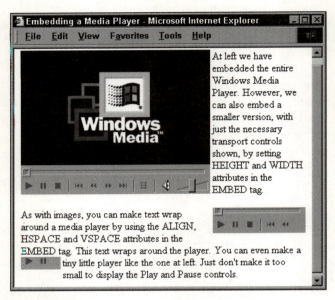

Figure 24-1
Three media players embedded into a Web page by using the EMBED ele-ment. The top player is full size, and the other two have been whittled down to the desired size by using the HEIGHT and WIDTH attributes.

20 Min. To Go

Applications of Web Audio and Video

Audio is becoming fairly common on the Web. Sites use audio for various different purposes. The best way to include an audio file, and the best format to use, depends on the particular application.

- *Welcome message.* Plays once when a page is loaded; because some users find audio intrusive, this and other audio applications that play automatically are seldom used. If you must, you can include an audio file that plays automatically on page load by using an EMBED tag with the attributes HIDDEN="true" and AUTOSTART="true".

- *Background track.* Plays continuously when a user is on a particular site; few sites use background tracks, and I don't recommend them. MIDI background tracks are considered particularly obnoxious.

- *Clickable sound effect.* Allows a user to click a link and hear a sound; a common example is a language instruction site, which might allow users to click a foreign word to hear a native speaker pronounce it. The best way to do this is with the A tag, using an ordinary `.wav` or `.aiff` file. Assuming that the sound in question is short, there's no real need to use streaming.

- *Action-based sound effect.* Makes a sound when a user performs an action such as moving the mouse over a navbar element; this is done using scripting, and you learn to do it in Session 26.

- *Downloadable audio or video file.* Enables users to download an audio or video file and store it on their local hard disks; this is common on music sites. For audio, `.mp3` is the best format to use because of its small file size and good (near-CD) quality.

- *Streaming audio or video file.* Enables users to play a file over the Internet but *not* to make a local copy; thus, streaming handily sidesteps copyright issues and makes live Internet broadcasts possible. You can link to a streaming file by using the Anchor (A) or EMBED tags. Use streaming any time you want to offer a sound file that's more than two or three seconds in duration.

Video is less common than audio on Web sites, mainly because of its higher bandwidth requirements. Technically, you can substitute video for audio in any of the applications listed in the preceding section. Practically speaking, however, few sites want to use a video clip as a welcome message or as a clickable or action-based effect. There are many useful applications of video on the Web, including online training, live news feeds, music videos and movie trailers. For most video applications, the best choice is simply to offer a video clip as either a downloadable file or as a streaming file.

In many cases, it's good to offer your site visitors a choice of file formats. Streaming media can be encoded at several quality levels to accommodate users who have different types of Internet connections. Offer a low-quality, fast-loading version for users who have dial-up connections and a higher-quality version for those fortunate souls using cable modems or DSL. Streaming-media encoders (described later in this session) make it easy to create several alternate versions of a streaming file. Also, some people prefer to download files, while others prefer streaming. Therefore, many sites offer users a choice of a downloadable file or a streaming file.

**10 Min.
To Go**

Software for Web Audio and Video

You need special software to play and create audio and video files. Fortunately, a wide range of free and easy-to-use tools is available.

Media players

A software application that enables you to play audio and video is called a *media player*. A media player can act as a plug-in with a browser, or it can be used on its own without a browser. It can play back various types of media files either on a local system or over the Internet.

At the moment, three products dominate the media-player market:

1. *Windows Media Player*. By Microsoft. See http://www.microsoft.com/windows/windowsmedia/.
2. *Real Player*. By RealNetworks. See http://www.real.com/player/.
3. *QuickTime Player*. By Apple. See http://www.apple.com/quicktime/.

All three products support all common audio and video file formats, run on either Windows or Mac, and offer downloadable free versions. So, marketing aside, there's little reason for a user to choose one over the other. Each of the three players has its own native media format, but nowadays they all support each others' formats as well as most of the other formats discussed in Session 23.

Media encoders and editors

Recording and editing audio and video is not really something that falls within the field of Web design, but Web site developers often find it necessary to prepare existing audio and video files for use on the Web. This may involve changing some of the file parameters to reduce file size, as discussed in Session 23, as well as converting the media to a Web-friendly format.

Each of the "big three" offers its own *media encoder*, an application that enables you to convert audio and video files to streaming formats such as Windows Media Format (Windows Media Encoder), RealMedia (RealProducer Plus) and QuickTime (QuickTime Pro).

These encoders incorporate some basic editing functions. If you need more sophisticated editing features, and especially if you're producing your own media from scratch, you may want to buy one of the various professional audio editors offered by Sonic Foundry (http://www.sonicfoundry.com/), Cakewalk (http://www.cakewalk.com/), or Cubase (http://www.cubase.com/). For video editing, Premiere 6.0 from Adobe (http://www.adobe.com/) has long been the most popular application.

REVIEW

Done!

In this session, you have learned to add audio and video to a Web site. This has included:

- Linking to an audio or video file by using the A and EMBED tags
- Preferred techniques and formats for different audio and video applications
- Audio and video software

QUIZ YOURSELF

1. What are two tags you can use to insert audio or video into a Web page? (See "Including Audio or Video in a Web Page.")

2. What is the advantage of using the EMBED tag? (See "Including Audio or Video in a Web Page.")

3. If you want to offer audio files for users to download to their local hard drives, what's the best format to use? (See "Applications of Web Audio and Video.")

4. What are two reasons that you might want to offer site users a choice of audio formats? (See "Applications of Web Audio and Video.")

5. What's the difference between a media player and a media encoder? (See "Software for Web Audio and Video.")

Using Scripting to Make Your Pages More Interactive

Session Checklist

✔ Adding scripting to a Web page

✔ Using the NAME attribute

✔ Changing an image's appearance in response to mouse movement

**30 Min.
To Go**

I n Session 1, you learn that HTML is a markup language, not a programming language. HTML can be used to specify how a page containing text and images is to be presented, but it cannot, by itself, be used to write a program that *performs an action*. To give a Web page the ability to perform an action (that is, to accept input, process data, and generate output), you need to use scripting.

In Session 16, you are introduced to CGI scripts, which run on the Web server and, therefore, are called *server-side* scripts. In this session, you learn about another type of scripting called *JavaScript*. JavaScript enables you to create *client-side* scripts, which run locally in the Web browser. The advantage of client-side scripting is that it allows you to provide real-time interactive features. The browser can respond to user actions instantly without having to send a message to the Web server.

Including Scripting in a Web Page

Like style sheets, scripting can be included in a Web page in three ways:

1. Apply scripting to an individual element by including scripting within
    a tag.

2. Apply scripting to an entire HTML document by including a SCRIPT ele-
    ment within the HEAD section. For example:

    ```
    <SCRIPT LANGUAGE="JavaScript">

    <!--

    Example script here.

    -->

    </SCRIPT>
    ```

3. Apply scripting to a group of documents by creating a text file that con-
    tains a script and including a link to that file in each document. A
    JavaScript file must have a .js extension and is referenced by using the
    SRC attribute in the SCRIPT tag, for example:

    ```
    <SCRIPT LANGUAGE="JavaScript" SRC="scripts/script.js">
    ```

Creating Rollover Buttons

The key to creating interactive elements by using JavaScript is an *event*. An event
is something that happens on a Web page, usually as a result of something the
user does, such as moving the mouse, clicking a link, or entering data into a form.
An *event handler* causes a bit of JavaScript code to be executed when the specified
event occurs. An event handler can exist within an HTML tag, and it can manipulate the attributes of other elements.

JavaScript recognizes many possible events. Three that have to do with the
user's mouse movements are:

*   onclick. Occurs when the user clicks a particular element
*   onmouseover. Occurs when the user moves the mouse over the element
*   onmouseout. Occurs when the user moves the mouse away from the
    element

For example, if we want to create a text hyperlink that does something cool when the user clicks it, we use the following HTML code:

```
<A onclick="function1()" HREF="saltwater.html">Click here</A>
```

When the user clicks this hyperlink, function1 does whatever it is function1 does. Naturally, the user is taken to the saltwater.html page.

JavaScript doesn't work on old legacy browsers (prior to about version 4.0).

20 Min. To Go

The NAME attribute

In Session 16, you learn that an input element in a form must be given a name to enable it to pass values to a script. In fact, you can include the NAME attribute in any HTML element to create a unique identifier for that element. If you want to be able to manipulate an element by using JavaScript, you must give it a unique name by using the NAME attribute.

For example:

```
<IMG SRC="images/navbar_salt.gif" BORDER="0" NAME="salt">
```

Now that we've given this image element a name, we can use a JavaScript event handler to manipulate its attributes.

```
OnMouseOver="salt.border='1'"
```

This event handler specifies that when the OnMouseOver event occurs, the element named salt has its BORDER attribute set to a value of 1. Note the use of single quotes *and* double quotes. An event handler is analogous to an attribute of the HTML tag in which it appears. Like the value of an attribute, the code that is triggered by an event handler appears within double quotes. Unlike a typical attribute, this code within the double quotes contains not one but three items:

1. The name of the element that is to be affected
2. The attribute of that element that is to be affected
3. The value to which that attribute is to be set. This value appears within single quotes.

You can create an image that changes its appearance, depending on whether the mouse is over it or not, by including event handlers for OnMouseOver and OnMouseOut in the IMG tag, as in Listing 25-1:

Listing 25-1:

```
<IMG SRC="images/navbar_salt.gif" BORDER="0" NAME="salt"
OnMouseOver="salt.border='1'" OnMouseOut="salt.border='0'">
```

In this example, the BORDER attribute of the IMG tag has a value of 0, so the image is displayed with no border when the page loads. When the user moves his or her mouse over the image, however, the first event handler sets the BORDER value to 1, and a 1-pixel border appears, as shown in Figure 25-1. When the user moves the mouse away again, the second event handler sets the BORDER value to 0, and the border disappears, as shown in Figure 25-2.

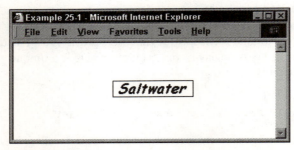

Figure 25-1
When the mouse is over the image, a border appears.

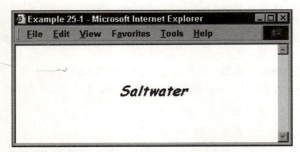

Figure 25-2
When the mouse is taken away, the border disappears.

**10 Min.
To Go**

Changing an image on mouseover

Not only the BORDER attribute but any possible attribute of a tag can be manipulated by using an event handler. If you manipulate the SRC attribute of the IMG
tag, you can cause a different image to be loaded in response to mouse movements
(or in response to any other possible event).

To do this, you need to create two alternate versions of the button. The
OnMouseOver event causes the *active* version of the button to be loaded, and the
OnMouseOut event loads the *inactive* version.

Test this on one of the navbar buttons you have created in Session 22:

1. Launch your graphic editor, and open the master file (not the .gif) for
   one of your navbar buttons.

2. Change the fill color to something that contrasts with the existing color.
   Freddy changes his from dark blue to red.

3. Save this file as a .gif, giving it a name that's similar to the name of the
   existing button. For example, Freddy's button is navbar_salt.gif, so he
   names this alternate version navbar_salt2.gif.

4. Insert the following code into an HTML file:
   ```
   <IMG SRC="images/navbar_salt.gif"
   BORDER="0" NAME="salt"
   OnMouseOver="salt.src='images/navbar_salt2.gif'"
   OnMouseOut="salt.src='images/navbar_salt.gif'">
   ```

5. The blue button changes to red when you move your mouse over it.
   What's happening is this: when the page first loads, the image specified
   in the SRC attribute (navbar_salt.gif) is loaded as usual. When a
   mouseover event occurs, the alternate image (navbar_salt2.gif) is
   loaded instead. When a mouseout event occurs, the original image is
   loaded again.

Freddy thinks this effect looks pretty nifty, so he adds this scripting to all the
buttons on his navbar.

Done!

REVIEW

In this session, you have learned:

- To add scripting to a Web page in three ways
- To give elements a NAME attribute so that you can manipulate them with scripting
- To create buttons that respond to mouse movement

QUIZ YOURSELF

1. What are three ways to apply scripting to a Web page? (See "Including Scripting in a Web Page.")

2. What are three events that have to do with mouse movement? (See "Creating Rollover Buttons.")

3. What is the purpose of giving an element a name? (See "The NAME Attribute.")

4. What is the result of the following JavaScript code: OnClick="bob. border='5'" (See "The NAME Attribute.")

5. If you want an image to change to a different image when the mouse moves over it, what attribute do you manipulate? (See "Changing an Image on Mouseover.")

More Scripting Techniques

Session Checklist

✔ Enabling mouse events to trigger sounds

✔ Using scripting tastefully

✔ Learning other common scripting applications

**30 Min.
To Go**

In Session 25, you learn to make page elements respond to user actions by using JavaScript. In this session, you learn some other applications of scripting, and consider the important question of when it is appropriate to add scripting to a page.

Attaching Sounds to Mouse Events

Changing an image's appearance is only one of many things that mouse events and other user actions can trigger. Mouse movement can trigger sound. In the following example, we embed a sound in a Web page by using the EMBED tag; then we insert an event handler in an IMG tag that causes the sound to play on when the mouse moves over the image.

In Session 24, you learn that if you embed a sound in a Web page, and specify HIDDEN="true" in the EMBED element, the user doesn't see any transport controls. But doesn't this mean that the user has no way to play the sound? Not necessarily, because the sound file is still available to be triggered by scripting.

In Session 22, you build a navbar out of individual graphic buttons. In Session 25, you use JavaScript to make a border around each button appear when the mouse is over the button. Now we'll make the buttons bark on mouseover.

1. Open Listing 22-1, which contains a set of IMG elements arranged as a side navbar.

2. Embed a sound in the page by adding the following code:

```
<EMBED SRC = "dog_bark.wav"
HIDDEN = "true"
AUTOSTART = "false"
NAME = "bark"
>
```

Remember that you *must* give this element a unique name by specifying a value for the NAME attribute to be able to control it by using scripting.

The sound file dog_bark.wav **is on the CD-ROM in the** html_examples **directory. For this example, however, any short sound file will do.**

3. Add a JavaScript event handler to each IMG tag as follows:

```
<IMG SRC="images/navbar_salt.gif"
OnMouseOver="javascript:document.bark.play()">
```

4. Now when you move the mouse over each button, you hear a dog bark.

Using Scripting Tastefully

**20 Min.
To Go**

Freddy has done some pretty fancy things with his navbar. He's made the buttons turn from blue to red when you move the mouse over them, and even made them bark. Then Freddy asks himself, "Does all this stuff really make my Fishing Guide more useful?" The answer is no. Fortunately, when you're designing for the Web, it's easy to try new techniques and to abandon them if they don't work out.

Freddy decides that he does like the effect of the mouseover making a border appear. It reinforces the idea that the navbar buttons are clickable, and it may encourage people to check out the various sections of his site. But the other stuff, cute though it may be, serves no practical purpose. After all, what does a dog's bark have to do with fish?

So Freddy settles on the final version of his navbar, with the fairly subdued "appearing- border" effect, as shown in Listing 26-1:

Listing 26-1:

```
<DIV CLASS="sidebar">

<BR><BR><BR><BR>

<A HREF="index.html" OnMouseOver="home.border='1'"
OnMouseOut="home.border='0'"><IMG
NAME="home" SRC="../freds_fishing_guide/images/navbar_home.gif"
WIDTH="120" HEIGHT="24" BORDER="0" ALT="Return to the Home
Page"></A>
<BR>

<A HREF="saltwater.html" OnMouseOver="salt.border='1'"
OnMouseOut="salt.border='0'"><IMG
NAME="salt" SRC="../freds_fishing_guide/images/navbar_salt.gif"
WIDTH="120" HEIGHT="24" BORDER="0" ALT="Saltwater Fishing"></A>
<BR>

<A HREF="freshwater.html" OnMouseOver="fresh.border='1'"
OnMouseOut="fresh.border='0'"><IMG
NAME="fresh" SRC="../freds_fishing_guide/images/navbar_fresh.gif"
WIDTH="120" HEIGHT="24" BORDER="0" ALT="Freshwater Fishing"></A>
<BR>
```

Continued

Listing 26-1   *Continued*

```
<A HREF="survey.html" OnMouseOver="survey.border='1'"
OnMouseOut="survey.border='0'"><IMG
NAME="survey"
SRC="../freds_fishing_guide/images/navbar_survey.gif" WIDTH="120"
HEIGHT="24" BORDER="0" ALT="Take our reader survey"></A>
<BR>

<A HREF="feedback.html" OnMouseOver="feed.border='1'"
OnMouseOut="feed.border='0'"><IMG
NAME="feed"
SRC="../freds_fishing_guide/images/navbar_feedback.gif"
WIDTH="120" HEIGHT="24" BORDER="0" ALT="Take our reader
survey"></A>
<BR>

</DIV>
```

Note a couple of things about this example:

1. Each of the individual images that make up the navbar must have its own unique name, which is referred to by both the mouseover and mouseout event handlers.

2. This time, we've placed the event handlers in the A element instead of the IMG element. The element to be manipulated by an event handler is referred to by its own unique name, so the event handler doesn't have to be in the element itself. In this particular example, the JavaScript event handler can be in either the IMG tag or the A tag.

Figure 26-1 shows Freddy's updated home page, complete with rollover navbar buttons.

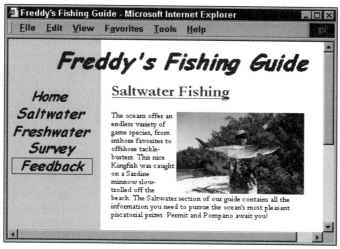

Figure 26-1
Using JavaScript, we've created a set of rollover buttons. When the mouse is over a particular button, a border appears.

**10 Min.
To Go**

Other Applications of Client-side Scripting

The techniques you've just learned scratch only the surface of what you can do with scripting. *Dynamic HTML* refers to the powerhouse combination of HTML, CSS, and scripting, which enables you to treat HTML elements as programmable objects that can change their content, their formatting, and even their positioning in response to many types of events.

Remember that *any* HTML element can be manipulated by scripting once you give the element a unique name by using the NAME attribute. Any property of that element you can define using CSS can be modified in real time by any of the events that JavaScript (or another scripting language) recognizes. Refer to a comprehensive dynamic HTML reference to get an idea of the endless possibilities.

Appendix C on the CD-ROM contains links to several online HTML reference sites.

JavaScript is powerful and complex; skill is required to write your own scripts. However, you don't need a lot of programming knowledge to add some simple scripting to your Web pages. Resources such as JavaScript.com (`http://www.javascript.com/`) and JavaScript Source (`http://javascript.internet.com/`) offer all kinds of scripts you can copy free and use in your own pages. You need to modify such scripts to suit your purposes, which should be easy enough with the basic knowledge of JavaScript you've obtained in these two sessions.

Some other common applications of scripting are:

- *Redirection*. A script can cause a specific page to be loaded automatically in response to an event. A *redirect* occurs when a request for a certain page causes another page to be loaded in its stead. For example, suppose you move your site to another server that has a different domain name. You can set up a redirect so that anyone who goes to the former address is taken automatically to the new one.

- *Browser checking*. A script can obtain various types of information about a Web- page visitor and can take action based on that information. For example, a browser-checking script can find out what brand and version of browser a particular visitor is using. If it's an older browser that doesn't support CSS, the script can trigger a redirect that sends the user to an alternate non-CSS version of the site.

- *Form validation*. In Session 16, you learn to collect data from users by using online forms. Human nature being what it is, users often enter invalid information, making the data useless. For example, let's say a user places an order for a product using a form. Unfortunately, they enter their credit card number incorrectly, and they fail to give you an email address or phone number. You can't contact them to get the right credit card number, so you've lost a sale.

  Scripting can *validate* user input in real time (that is, it can compare what users type against a database of valid responses and can show them error messages if they make mistakes). In the previous example, a script could have prevented them from submitting their order until they entered an email address. It could also verify that what they enter is a valid email address, by making sure it contains an @ symbol.

- *Password protection*. If you want to make a section of your site accessible to registered users only, scripting is one way to do it. However, a skilled programmer can defeat JavaScript password protection fairly easily, so it isn't used for heavy-duty security applications.

Done!

REVIEW

In this session, you have continued learning about scripting techniques:

- Attaching sounds to events
- Using scripting in a tasteful way
- Using client-side scripting for additional purposes

QUIZ YOURSELF

1. What JavaScript event handler can you use to cause a sound file to play? (See "Attaching Sounds to Mouse Events.")

2. If you want to use mouse movement to trigger a sound, what element must be included in the Web page in addition to the element that triggers the sound? (See "Attaching Sounds to Mouse Events.")

3. What question should you ask to determine whether you should include a particular scripting (or any other) technique in your Web site? (See "Using Scripting Tastefully.")

4. What is Dynamic HTML? (See "Other Applications of Client-side Scripting.")

5. Name at least three common uses of client-side scripting. (See "Other Applications of Client-side Scripting.")

P A R T

V

Sunday Morning

1. What is an animated `.gif` made up of?

2. The transparent `.gif` format isn't recommended for ad banners. Why not?

3. How does a `.gif` animation differ from a Flash animation?

4. If a user visits a page containing a Flash animation but the user's browser doesn't have the Flash plug-in installed, what happens?

5. Why should you keep copies of graphic files in your graphic editor's native format as well as in `.gif` or `.jpg` format?

6. What two elements do you use to define an image map?

7. Name three parameters of a digital audio file that affect file size.

8. What are the values of these parameters for CD-quality audio?

9. What is streaming media?

10. Name two tags you can use to include audio in a Web page.

11. Some sites offer site users a choice of audio formats. Why?

12. What does a media player do? What does a media encoder do?

13. What are three ways you can apply scripting to a Web page?

14. Name three events that have to do with mouse movement.

15. What must an HTML element have before it can be manipulated by scripting?

16. What is the result of the following JavaScript code?
    `OnMouseOver="button.src='image2.gif'"`

17. What JavaScript code can you use to cause a sound file to play?

18. What question must you ask yourself before deciding whether to include a particular scripting (or any other) technique in your Web site?

19. Name at least three common uses of client-side scripting.

20. Explain the concept of Dynamic HTML.

PART

VI

Sunday
Afternoon

Maintaining and Promoting a Web Site

Session Checklist

✔ Site testing and maintenance

✔ Making your site search-engine friendly

✔ Tracking your site visitors

**30 Min.
To Go**

One huge advantage the Web has over other media is that making changes to a Web site is easy and costs nothing. But a good Web site is never truly finished. Content needs to be updated; site features can be improved, and new opportunities arise to promote the site.

Testing and Troubleshooting

I can't say enough about the importance of thoroughly testing your site before you *launch* it (officially open it to your users). Test every link on every page several times, being especially thorough with any forms or scripting. Check out how your pages look with various window sizes and various screen resolutions.

How far you go to insure browser compatibility is up to you. At the least, you should test your pages with the latest versions of Internet Explorer (5.5) and

Netscape (6.0), as well as with one or more earlier versions of each. Remember that versions of IE and Netscape prior to 4.0 can't handle advanced CSS or JavaScript. If you really want your pages to look good on all systems, test them with several browser versions, including the lesser-known brands such as Opera, on both Windows and Mac, as well as on AOL.

 Appendix D on this book's CD-ROM explains browser differences and other user-compatibility issues.

Even once a site is launched, you should visit it once in a while and check that all the features are still working correctly. Encourage your users to send you e-mail to report any errors or bugs they find.

If something isn't working the way it's supposed to, *troubleshoot* the process by breaking it down into its components. For example, let's say you have placed an image on a page, but the image doesn't appear. Look at the step-by-step process by which the image file should load, and try to get each step to work individually:

1. View the image by itself in a browser or a graphic editor (you learn to use graphic editing software in Session 9). If the image file looks okay, you know it isn't the problem.

2. Check the file path the IMG element is using to link to the image file. If it's correct, you know the file path isn't the problem (you learn to create a link to an image file in Session 7, and you learn the intricacies of file addressing in Session 20).

3. Check the IMG tag itself, and any other HTML code that applies to the image. If another image on the same page works, temporarily replace the problem code with the working code. If it works, the problem must be the HTML code.

Good Coding Practice: The Comment Tag

The handy Comment tag is different from the other tags you've learned to use. It has no effect on the appearance of a Web page — that's the whole point. Whatever you place in a Comment tag is hidden from the browser and isn't displayed on the Web page.

```
<!-- This text is not displayed on the Web page. It's hidden. -->
```

Note that the Comment tag is a single tag that begins with `<!--` and ends with `-->`. Every programmer knows the value of *commenting* in computer code. Including some short explanatory remarks in your code can be very helpful to anyone who might need to edit your documents in the future — including you.

In Session 2, you learn to make your code easier to read by using indents and line breaks to set off various sections. This practice and the liberal use of comments are signs of a skilled coder.

You can use comment tags to make a note of the date on which you revise a file. This is a wise policy, especially if more than one person may be making changes to a file. For example:

```
<!-- This file revised by C.M. 5/1/01 -->
```

Comment tags have another use. You can use them to hide code from older browsers that don't support newer features of HTML. Many legacy browsers (previous to version 4.0 or so) don't support JavaScript or CSS. Fortunately, a browser ignores any code it doesn't understand, but there is still a danger that some of the code might be displayed on the Web page. By hiding your scripting or style-sheet code inside a comment tag, you can avoid this problem.

Note how we use a comment tag to enclose the body of the script:

```
<SCRIPT LANGUAGE="JavaScript">
<!--
Here is the body of the script.
-->
</SCRIPT>
```

**20 Min.
To Go**

Making Your Pages Search-engine Friendly

The majority of Web site visitors find sites through a search engine or online directory. Search sites such as Yahoo (`http://www.yahoo.com`); Excite (`http://www.Excite.com`); Altavista (`http://www.Altavista.com`); Google (`http://www.Google.com`); and the Open Directory (`http://dmoz.org`) are important online resources. If you want people to visit your site, it's important to be listed on as many major search sites as possible.

Some search sites use *spiders*, computer programs that continually search the Web for new sites and automatically add them to the search site's database; other search sites include only those sites whose owners request to be listed, offering an online form for the purpose. Submitting a new site to the search engines and directories is important, and I recommend that you approach the process carefully and thoroughly (once your site is launched and ready for visitors, of course).

Properly submitting a site can be an involved process, and there's no room to describe it fully here. Selfpromotion.com (`http://Selfpromotion.com`), GetSubmitted.com (`http://www.getsubmitted.com/`), and Search Engine Watch (`http://www.SearchEngineWatch.com`) each have a wealth of information about search sites and Web site promotion. Yahoo's Site Announcement and Promotion category (`http://dir.yahoo.com/Computers_and_Internet/Internet/World_Wide_Web/Site_Announcement_and_Promotion/`) contains a huge list of relevant resources.

Proper submission is an ongoing process. After site launch and your initial submission, you should revisit the major search sites periodically to make sure your listing is still present and up to date. However, there are a couple of things you should keep in mind as you design your site so that the search engines index it properly.

Writing a user-friendly, descriptive TITLE tag

Most or all search engines use the `TITLE` tag as an important indicator of the content of a page. Also, if a user adds one of your pages to his or her list of Favorites (or Bookmarks), the `TITLE` appears in the Favorites list. So be sure each page has a `TITLE` that accurately and concisely describes the page's content.

Every page title should contain:

1. The name of the site
2. The name of the individual page
3. A brief description of the page's contents

For example, here's the `TITLE` from Freddy's home page:

```
<TITLE>Freddy's Fishing Guide: Free information about the best
fishing spots, tackle and techniques.</TITLE>
```

Here's the `TITLE` from the Saltwater hub page:

```
<TITLE>Saltwater Fish (Freddy's Fishing Guide)</TITLE>
```

Here's the TITLE from the Freshwater hub page:

```
<TITLE>Freshwater Fish (Freddy's Fishing Guide)</TITLE>
```

Describing your content by using META tags

You can use META tags to identify information *about* an HTML document, such as the document's title, author, date of publication, and so forth. This information is not displayed on the Web page, but can be read by spiders. There are two types of META tags that some search engines use to categorize Web sites: the META "description" and META "keywords" tags. Like the TITLE tag, these tags are included in the HEAD section, and their form is as follows:

```
<META NAME="description" CONTENT="Your source for the latest
fishing tips.">
<META NAME="keywords" CONTENT="fish, fishing, bass, trout,
billfish, kingfish, pargo">
```

The "description" tag contains a brief description of the page, similar to but not necessarily the same as that in the TITLE tag. The "keywords" tag contains a short list of *keywords* that relate to the page's subject matter. To find appropriate keywords, try to think of words that a Web surfer might type into a search engine if he or she were looking for a site like yours.

Contrary to the claims of many Web hucksters, these two META tags are not magical formulas for drawing huge numbers of visitors to your site. They're just another tool to enable search engines to index and categorize your pages appropriately. Keep them short and to the point.

Search engines use keywords to rank pages, so some site owners reason that the more instances of a certain keyword a page has, the higher that page ranks in search results. This leads some overzealous souls to include excessively long lists of keywords in TITLE or META tags or as invisible text. Don't do it! The search engines became wise to these tricks years ago, and they'll bar your site if they suspect you of "spamming" their database. Any use whatsoever of invisible text gets you barred from most search engines. And don't use keywords that aren't related to your site content.

**10 Min.
To Go**

Measuring Site Traffic

Once your site is launched, you'll probably want to know who is visiting it. For a business site, any information you can get about your site users is valuable because you can use it to gauge not only your site's overall effectiveness but the effectiveness of individual site features and of your marketing efforts.

All Web servers can keep a log of every file request to the server. These *server logs* contain all sorts of information about the people who are visiting your site. To make use of this gold mine of information, instruct your hosting service to enable server logging for your site and to give you access to the log files. The log files themselves are a bit too lengthy and cryptic to be read directly, but many software products can analyze them for you and can prepare a detailed and readable report. Such *log analysis* (or *traffic analysis*) software packages range from Analog (`http://www.statslab.cam.ac.uk/~sret1/analog/`), a free tool available for every operating system under the Sun, to high-dollar corporate products, such as WebTrends Enterprise Suite.

Many hosting services make basic log analysis software available to their clients. In fact, your hosting service may be able to arrange for you to receive a weekly report by e-mail on your site traffic so you don't have to deal directly with the server logs.

Here's some of the information you can get from your server logs and how you can use it to improve your Web site:

- *Overall site traffic.* By measuring your traffic over time, you can see if it's growing (let's hope so), holding steady, or declining. In addition, you can roughly measure the effectiveness of any advertising or other marketing you do by seeing whether it causes a spike in traffic.

- *Most/least visited pages.* This can identify your most and least popular site features and can indicate the content areas you are strong in and those that need improvement.

- *Top referring sites.* This tells you where your traffic is coming from. You can use it to see which search engines are sending you the most traffic and to assess the value of any reciprocal links you may have with other sites.

- *User browsers and operating systems.* This can tell you how many of your users have the latest browsers and how many are using old legacy browsers. It can also tell you the relative proportions of Windows, Mac and Unix users among your visitors. Armed with this information, you can judge how much you need to tailor your site design or content for different types of user systems.

● *Error log.* A certain number of failed page requests is inevitable, but this number should be only a tiny fraction of the successful requests. If you see a high number of failed requests, it can indicate an error on your site or a problem with the hosting service. It can mean that your pages take too long to load so that visitors are bailing out before pages are fully loaded.

Done!

REVIEW

This session has discussed several issues involving site maintenance and promotion. This has included:

● Testing and maintaining a site
● Optimizing a site for the search engines
● Recording and analyzing site-traffic data

QUIZ YOURSELF

1. What is involved in troubleshooting a Web page? (See "Testing and Troubleshooting.")
2. Name at least one use of the comment tag. (See "Good Coding Practice: The Comment Tag.")
3. What should the TITLE tag of a page include? (See " Writing a User-friendly, Descriptive TITLE Tag.")
4. What two META tags help search engines index your site? (See "Describing your Content by using META Tags.")
5. What is the name of the file that keeps a record of every file request to a Web server? (See "Measuring Site Traffic.")

Exploring Dynamic Page Generation

Session Checklist

✔ Understanding dynamic page generation

✔ Delivering content dynamically by using Server-side Includes

✔ Exploring dynamic scripting tools

You have learned that when a browser requests a Web page, the server delivers an HTML file that contains both content and formatting. However, there is another way to serve Web pages: dynamic page generation.

*30 Min.
To Go*

Understanding Dynamic Web Content

Freddy's Fishing Guide, like many Web sites, is a *static* site. This means that the HTML pages that make up the site have been created ahead of time and are sitting on the server's hard drive, waiting for someone to request them. No matter who requests a page, or when the person requests it, the server retrieves that page from its hard drive and delivers it.

For most sites, especially smaller ones, there's no problem with this arrangement. Some sites, however, choose to use *dynamic page generation*. When a user requests a page on a *dynamic site*, a script assembles various components into a complete HTML page and delivers it to the user. For example, the content of a Web page might be stored in one file and the HTML tags that specify its formatting in a separate file. When a user requests the page, a script on the server merges the two files into one and serves it to the user.

Figure 28-1 shows the process of serving a static Web page; Figure 28-2 shows dynamic Web-page delivery.

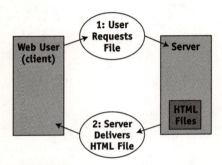

Figure 28-1
Static Web-page delivery

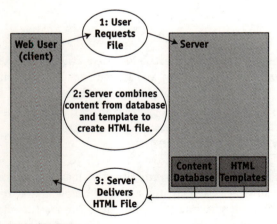

Figure 28-2
Dynamic Web-page delivery

Note

***Dynamic* is used by different people to mean different things, but in this context it refers solely to the practice of creating Web pages at the time they are requested. Dynamic HTML, mentioned in Session 26, is a separate topic.**

Dynamic page generation is rapidly becoming more popular. Many of the Web's largest sites are dynamic sites. It's also common for a site to have both static and dynamic sections. There are several reasons why a site might want to use dynamic page generation:

- *Efficiency.* Usually, a large Web site has a lot of pages that use the same formatting but have different content. On a static site (also called a *flat* site), every HTML file must contain a duplicate of the elements that are common to every page (perhaps a navbar and a heading). On a dynamic site, the common elements need to be stored in only one file (a page template) and loaded only once per user session. This saves both server hard drive space and page-load time.

- *Database integration.* Many Web pages serve as the front end for some sort of database. For example, imagine a store that has a product database it wants to make available on the Web. The store's Web site designer can create an HTML page for each record in the database, but this is tedious and inefficient; in addition, it requires a new HTML page to be generated and loaded to the Web server any time the information in the database changes. Dynamic page generation allows a Web server to retrieve content directly from a database, eliminating the need to store information in two places. Also, it enables users to create custom queries for a database.

- *Personalization.* Dynamic page generation can create a page that incorporates content specific to a particular user. You've learned that client-side scripts can obtain certain information about a particular user, such as the browser and operating system he or she is using. There are various other ways for a site to gather information about its users (including voluntary user surveys like the one on Freddy's site). A dynamic page generation system can use this information to deliver custom-tailored content. For example, if the system can tell that a certain visitor is using a Mac, it can deliver special Mac-related content.

- *User-created content.* Many sites allow visitors to contribute, or *post*, their own content. An online discussion group, which allows users to post comments and to reply to others' posts, is one example. You can create your own interactive discussion groups by using a special kind of dynamic page generation software. Several such products are available, and your hosting service may even have one available for you to use.

Appendix C on the accompanying CD-ROM contains the Web addresses of a couple of online discussion groups. These groups are not only valuable sources of information on their respective topics but can serve as models of how a discussion group is set up.

20 Min.
To Go

Using Server-side Includes

Server-side Includes (SSI) is a feature of many Web servers that enables you to insert various types of data dynamically into a Web page. SSI can do some of the things JavaScript can do, such as returning information about a user's browser, current time, and so on.

Many popular Web server software packages offer SSI as a built-in feature. However, it's not available on all servers. Ask your hosting service if you can use SSI.

Using SSI is the simplest way to insert an external file into an HTML page. You can use this feature of SSI to create semi-dynamic pages. To include a file in a Web page, simply place this code at the desired insertion point:

```
<!--#include virtual="file.html"-->
```

Note that the SSI appears within a Comment tag. The referenced file (file.html, in this example) can be any HTML file, but be sure to specify the file path correctly.

You learn about the Comment tag in Session 27. Perhaps the Comment tag is misnamed since, as you have learned, you can use it for several things in addition to inserting comments into your code.

As an example of dynamic page generation, consider Freddy's navbar. The navbar is a lengthy piece of code that's exactly the same on every page of the site and thus a good candidate for dynamic generation. You can convert the navbar to dynamic delivery as follows:

1. Open `freds_fishing_guide_advanced/index.html` in your Web editor.

2. Find the section of code that creates the sidebar. This is the section between the two comment tags:

    ```
    <!-- Beginning of Sidebar -->
    ```

    and

    ```
    <!-- End of Sidebar -->
    ```

    Those comment tags are handy, aren't they?

3. Select all the code between these two comment tags; cut the code from the file (Ctrl+X), and paste it into a new file (Ctrl+V).

4. Save the new file as `sidebar.html` in a new directory called `includes`. This file should contain *only* the code that creates the sidebar (no HTML, HEAD, or BODY tags).

5. Return to the `freds_fishing_guide_advanced/index.html` file. Where the sidebar code used to be, place the following code:

    ```
    <!--#include virtual="includes/sidebar.html"-->
    ```

6. Save this file under a new name, such as `index2.html`.

7. Load this file and the `includes` directory to a directory on your Web server.

8. When you view `index2.html` live on the server, it should appear identical to `index.html`. The finished page that's delivered to the browser is exactly the same. The difference is that, using static delivery, the page exists on the server's hard drive in its complete form (`index.html`); using dynamic delivery, the page is assembled in real time from two separate files (`index2html` and `sidebar.html`).

As the name implies, Server-side Includes happen on the server. If you use SSI in a page, you can't see the effect of the SSI when you preview the page on your local system; to test pages that use SSI, they must be live on the server.

Of course, a site as small as Freddy's Fishing Guide has no real need for dynamic page generation. However, this simple application of SSI should be a good example of how dynamic page generation works.

Dynamic Scripting Tools

SSI is handy, but it's a partial solution rather than a tool for building a fully dynamic site. Because each SSI element must make its own file request to the server, using too many SSI elements can hurt your page-load time. If you want to make a section or two of a site dynamic, SSI is a simple (and free) way to do it. But if you aim to build an entirely dynamic site, you'll want to check out the more sophisticated dynamic scripting tools.

As explained previously in this session, a server-side script performs dynamic page generation. The user's page request triggers the script, which decides what components to use, puts them together, and delivers the resulting Web page. A page generation script can be written in any language and can be executed using CGI (as you learn in Session 16, CGI is a specification for transferring information between a Web page and a script).

The combination of CGI and the Perl scripting language is an old standby that's been used in many Web sites, but most developers consider it a bit old-fashioned, as it's slow and bandwidth intensive compared to more modern tools. Nowadays, many scripting environments are available that make it easy to incorporate dynamic page generation and other applications into a Web site, with a minimum of programming knowledge. Scripting tools range from open-source languages that are free for anyone to use to complex and pricey commercial software packages.

A scripting environment has two aspects: a set of special tags you can insert in your HTML pages to provide access to scripting functions; *server extensions*, which enable your Web server to recognize these tags.

One powerful free solution is PHP (officially called Hypertext Preprocessor, although this name is seldom used). This scripting language is open source, meaning that anyone can use it for free. Learn more about PHP at http://www.php.net. Microsoft's Active Server Pages (ASP), Java Server Pages (JSP) and Allaire's Cold Fusion are other popular scripting environments. Many hosting services make such scripting tools available for use on clients' sites, and it's likely that your hosting service has one or all of these tools.

Done!

REVIEW

In this session, you have learned a new way to serve Web pages: dynamic page generation. This has included:

- Understanding dynamic content
- Creating dynamic pages by using SSI
- Using other scripting tools

QUIZ YOURSELF

1. What happens when a user requests a dynamically generated Web page? (See "Understanding Dynamic Web Content.")

2. Name at least two reasons why a site might want to use dynamic page generation. (See "Understanding Dynamic Web Content.")

3. What HTML tag do you use to invoke an SSI? (See "Using Server-side Includes.")

4. What's the simplest way to insert an external file into an HTML page? (See "Using Server-side Includes.")

5. What are the two most popular commercial scripting solutions? What is a free alternative? (See "Dynamic Scripting Tools.")

SESSION

29

Overhauling a Web Site

Session Checklist

✔ Critiquing a site

✔ Creating a page layout in three ways

✔ Creating a navbar in three ways

**30 Min.
To Go**

As you've progressed through this book, you've learned many Web-design
techniques and have applied each to a sample Web site: the fictional
Freddy's Fishing Guide. However, the key to being a successful Web designer
is not just knowing *how* to use the various techniques but *when* to use them.

In this session, you'll see how you can make the Web site you've created in the
first two parts of the book more attractive and easier to use by applying some of
the advanced techniques you've learned in the later parts. This should help you
understand how these techniques can work together to create a functional site
that has a consistent look and feel.

Critiquing the Freddy's Fishing Guide Site

In addition to building new sites from scratch, Web designers are often called upon to revise and improve existing sites. Improvements to a Web site fall into two categories: appearance and utility. Every change you make should be intended either to make a page look nicer or to make the site serve its intended purpose better.

A more attractive page doesn't always mean a more complicated page. In fact, the reverse is often true. Elegant simplicity should be your goal.

The simple version of Freddy's site is in the `freds_fishing_guide` **directory on the accompanying CD-ROM.**

Look at the simple version of Freddy's home page, shown in Figure 29-1. For the work of a beginner, it's okay, but now that you're looking at it with a more experienced eye, you may perceive three weak points:

1. The column of text is pretty wide, at least if you're viewing the page with your browser window full-screen. It might be easier to read if the column were a little narrower. The whole page has a very linear look, with one element following another down the page in single file, though we have wrapped text around the two photos by using the `ALIGN` attribute, which helps a bit. In the early days of the Web, this rigid linear layout was typical, but there's no excuse for it now that we have tools such as tables and style sheets.

2. The home page doesn't give visitors an overview of what's available on the site. Only the link to the Saltwater section is visible above the fold (that is, visible without scrolling).

3. Because the code doesn't specify a typeface, this page is displayed with the browser default, Times New Roman. There's nothing wrong with this typeface, but every Web user has seen it thousands of times. Freddy's site might look a little more distinctive if it used a less common font. Another way to spice things up is to use two contrasting fonts for different text elements.

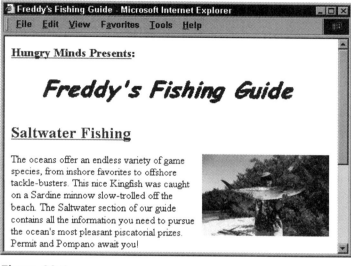

Figure 29-1
This page has been created by using the techniques described in the first two parts of the book. You can improve the page by applying some of the more advanced techniques from later sessions.

Improving Page Layout

**20 Min.
To Go**

By simply dividing Freddy's home page into two columns, we can solve problems 1 and 2. We can force the body text into a narrower column, and a left sidebar can provide a space where we can place links to all the site features.

You've learned three ways to divide a page into sections. In Session 12, you create a two-column layout by using tables (see Listing 12-1). In later sessions, you achieve similar results with both frames and divisions (in conjunction with CSS). Which way is best? The answer, of course, depends on what you're trying to achieve on a particular page.

CSS is preferable to tables for page-layout purposes for three reasons:

1. CSS allows more precise positioning.
2. Using tables can generate long and labyrinthine code. Style sheets do the job with far less code.

3. Using tables for positioning can cause problems for users who have dis-
    abilities and who may be using special browsers.

**Appendix D on the accompanying CD-ROM explains the issue of
making Web pages accessible to users who have disabilities.**

Frames are used to create sections of a page that can scroll independently of
one another. Unlike tables and divisions, frames aren't useful for precisely positioning objects. For dividing a page into columns, however, frames work fine and
have the added bonus that they can make a site a little faster, as not all of the
page elements have to reload with every page. A three-frame page layout like the
one you create in Session 14 works well for Freddy's site (see Listing 14-1).

In the end, however, Freddy decides that he likes the CSS-based layout that you
create for him in Session 19. He wants his site to be consistent, so he decides to
make every page use this layout. As you recall, this page layout uses three divisions: one for the heading, one for the left sidebar, and one for the right main column. Using one page as a template, simply paste the content for each page into
the maincol division, leaving the other two divisions the same. Alternatively, you
can use an SSI to insert the contents of the heading and sidebar divisions, as
you learn to do in Session 28.

**You can save yourself a lot of work, and ensure consistency, by
creating a page template. Save a file that contains all the elements you want every page to have, and use it as a model when
you create new pages.**

**10 Min.
To Go**

Fixing Freddy's Fonts

Freddy chooses Comic Sans MS as the font for his main heading, and he wants that
font for all his subheadings, too. After all, most designers frown on using more
than two fonts on a page. In Session 17, you create a style sheet that specifies one
font for headings and another for body text. Now Freddy modifies that to specify
Comic Sans MS as his top choice for a heading font, as follows:

```
H1, H2, H3, H4
    {
    color: #000088;
```

```
font-family: Comic Sans MS, Verdana, Arial, Helvetica, sans-
serif;
}
```

Note that font names must appear exactly the way they're listed on users' systems (just "Comic Sans" won't do). Of course, not all users have Comic Sans MS on their systems. Users who have it see the page exactly as intended, but those who don't see it with one of the other fonts listed, which hopefully won't look too bad. Even if you specify a special font, you should test your pages with default fonts to be sure that they look acceptable.

Choosing a Navbar

A navbar is an important element that serves several purposes. Having a consistent navbar on every page accomplishes the following:

- Reinforces the unique look of a site (branding)
- Shows users at a glance what's available on a site
- Helps users navigate back to the home page if they get lost

Because Freddy's site has only five pages, they're all listed on the navbar. Of course, a larger site's navbar includes only the main sectional hub pages, each of which might have several more specific pages below it.

A text navbar

In Listing 14-1, you create a navbar by using simple HTML text. There's nothing wrong with text navbars, and many sites use them. A text navbar loads faster than a graphic navbar and is easier to modify. You can create rollover effects for a text navbar (or any text, for that matter) just as you do for the graphic navbar in Session 25. Simply give each Anchor element a NAME; then you can manipulate the element's attributes by using scripting.

Graphic text buttons

In the first half of Session 22, you build a navbar from individual graphic buttons. The advantages of using graphic text instead of HTML text are that you can use any font you want, and you can combine pictures with the text. (But keep it simple!) Using individual buttons makes it easy to add or remove individual items if you change your site structure later.

A graphic navbar with an image map

Later in Session 22, you create a navbar consisting of a single graphic image that uses an image map to link to the various pages. A single-image navbar can be quite attractive, but is not as easy to modify later as a text navbar or a multiple-image navbar.

Figures 29-2, 29-3, and 29-4 show the three alternative versions of Freddy's navbar.

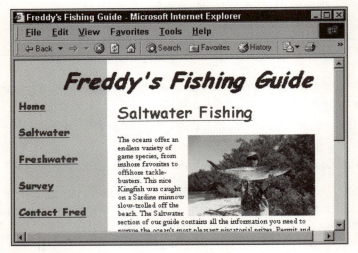

Figure 29-2

Freddy's home page with a text navbar

Which navbar is best? It's really a question of personal preference. Freddy decides that the text navbar looks too plain and that the navbar that uses the image map looks too fancy, so he goes with the "just right" navbar made up of individual buttons.

The Web makes it wonderfully easy to experiment with new features and different ways of doing things. Freddy has tried out a lot of different techniques on his site. He knows, however, that every goodie he adds to a page makes the page load a little slower and that fast-loading, trouble-free pages keep site visitors coming back. So every time he considers adding something, he asks himself, "Does this feature really make my site more useful?" If the answer is no, he leaves it out.

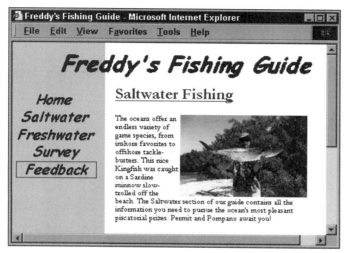

Figure 29-3
The page with a navbar made up of individual buttons

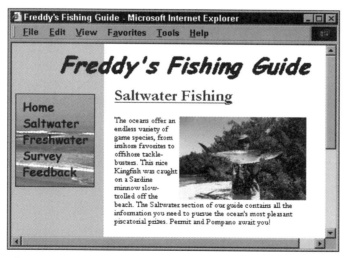

Figure 29-4
This navbar is made up of a single graphic, linked by using an image map.

Freddy's revised home page is shown in Figure 29-5.

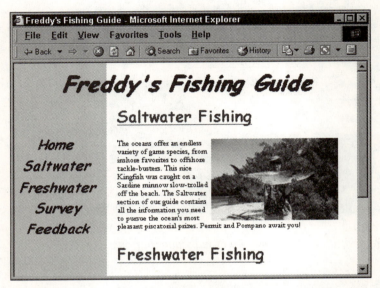

Figure 29-5
*The new and improved site is both more attractive and more functional
thanks to the discreet use of style sheets and scripting.*

The improved version of Freddy's site is in the directory
`freds_fishing_guide_advanced` **on the accompanying CD-ROM.**

What about the former version of Freddy's site? Freddy keeps it around as an
alternative site for users who have legacy browsers that don't support CSS or
JavaScript. He can offer a link to the alternative site, but an even better option is
to use a script that checks a user's browser version and automatically directs visitors who have pre-4.0 browsers to the alternative site.

**See Appendix C on the CD-ROM for a list of sites where you can
find browser-checking scripts.**

Done!

REVIEW

In this session, you have overhauled an example Web site, adding features that improve site appearance and usefulness. This has involved:

- Critiquing a Web site
- Creating a good page layout
- Choosing an appropriate navbar

QUIZ YOURSELF

1. What are two things about a Web page that might have room for improvement? (See "Critiquing the Freddy's Fishing Guide Site.")

2. What are three ways to divide a Web page into sections? (See "Improving Page Layout.")

3. What's the best way to position elements on a page? (See "Improving Page Layout.")

4. What are three reasons to have a consistent navbar on every page of a site? (See "Choosing a Navbar.")

5. What are three ways to create a navbar? (See "Choosing a Navbar.")

Go Forth and Multiply

Session Checklist

✔ Keeping quality design principles in mind

✔ Using existing Web pages as models

✔ Finding help with Web-design problems

**30 Min.
To Go**

Some Web sites are attractive, effective in their intended purpose, and pleasant to use. Far too many, however, are marred by poor organization, amateurish appearance, slow-loading pages, HTML that won't work in all browsers, and a host of other ills. Usually, the difference between the good sites and the bad is not any one major thing but the cumulative effect of dozens of tiny details.

Throughout this book, I've tried to present techniques that yield the best results, warning against quality-sacrificing shortcuts and pointing out areas in which you need to take special care to make your pages the best they can be. In this session, we combine these good design rules into a set of overall principles for you to keep in mind as you design, build, and maintain Web sites.

Principles of Quality Web Design

1. *Stay focused on your site goals.* This is the most important design principle of all. Every Web site is built for a particular purpose or purposes. Be clear about what those purposes are, and keep them in mind during every aspect of site development, from designing pages to creating a navigational scheme to choosing a hosting service. If you're selling something, be sure your site makes people want to buy. If your main goal is to distribute information, be sure that information is well presented and easy for users to get to. If something doesn't serve the overall goals of your site, *don't use it.*

2. *Keep it simple.* This is closely related to the previous rule. Fancy graphics, audio, clever scripting, and other bells and whistles cause pages to load more slowly and mean more work for you and possibly more hassles for your users. Use graphics and other features sparingly. *When in doubt, leave it out.*

3. *Try to think as your users do.* Are a lot of your users likely to be new to the Web? If so, don't assume that they understand how things such as hyperlinks work. Provide explanatory text, and make things painfully clear.

   Are people from outside the United States potential customers? If so, use simple English; avoid American colloquialisms, and make sure your online ordering system can handle foreign credit cards and foreign delivery addresses. These are just two examples of how you should put yourself in your users' place. Try to imagine who your users are, and ask yourself if they'll be able to figure out how to take full advantage of your site.

4. *Don't compromise on quality.* It's often possible to save money and/or time by cutting corners, but it's usually a mistake. The Web is becoming a familiar medium, and people expect attractive, professional-looking sites. Take time to ensure that your graphics look good and that your pages are attractively laid out.

5. *Be conscious of compatibility issues, but don't become obsessed by them.* Test your site with as many different systems and browser versions as you can, and try to ensure that it looks acceptable on all. It may be too much to hope that your site looks just right on some ancient legacy browser or obscure operating system, but strive to create pages that look great on current systems and acceptable on all systems. The more important it is

to you to reach technically-challenged users (that is, users with outdated or nonstandard software or networks), the more universal your pages should be.

Appendix D (CD-ROM only) contains a discussion of Web-compatibility issues.

6. *Carefully proof and troubleshoot your site.* It's amazing how many sites have dead links, features that don't work correctly, ludicrous typographical errors and other amateur blunders. As a site becomes more complex, it becomes easier and easier for minor errors to creep in. Seemingly minor errors, however, can have a shocking effect on a site's user traffic. Test *every* link and site feature repeatedly, live on the server, before making a page available to the public.

7. *Maintain your site.* One of the best things about the Web is that it makes it so easy to keep content up to the minute. Review your site regularly; revise any content that becomes out of date, and add new material often to keep visitors coming back.

Finding Help and Free Resources

20 Min. To Go

I hope this book has answered a lot of questions for you. If you're at all intrigued by the Web, however, I'm sure it has raised a lot of other questions. We've had time to cover various topics only briefly, so you may feel that you need more details on these topics.

Fortunately, a vast amount of information is online, available absolutely free, to help you in your further study of Web design. Once you're familiar with some of the resources available, you'll find that the answer to any HTML dilemma, CSS nightmare, or software snafu is never more than a few clicks away.

The companion CD-ROM contains a list of links to some of the Web's best free resource sites, only a few of which are listed here.

The sincerest form of flattery

One way to learn Web design techniques is to copy the code of existing pages. To learn how other designers approach page-design issues, surf the Web often, checking out as many sites as you can. If you see a page-design technique you like, copy the HTML code and replace the content with your own. Can't figure out how to do something? Find a site that is doing it successfully, and examine its code.

Here's how to do it:

1. Open the desired page in a Web browser.
2. In Internet Explorer, choose View ⇨ Source. In Netscape, choose View ⇨ Page Source. The source code of the page will be displayed.
3. Select the desired code, and copy it to the clipboard (Ctrl+C).
4. Launch your Web editor, and paste the code into an HTML file.

Isn't this copyright infringement? Not necessarily. Generally, HTML code is protected by copyright, but no one can copyright a common design technique, and one designer's sidebar table (for example) looks pretty much the same as another's. You can't copy the overall look and feel of a site without permission, but snitching small snippets of code and modifying them for your own use is generally considered okay.

 Copying content is an entirely different matter from copying code. All types of site content, including text, images, audio, and other media, are protected by copyright; copying them without permission is definitely illegal.

10 Min. To Go

Online magazines and tutorials

Online resources, such as the Web Developer family of online magazines (`http://webdeveloper.com`), contain step-by-step tutorials on every imaginable Web- design technique, searchable reference material (a comprehensive HTML reference makes an invaluable companion to this book), reviews of the latest Web design software, and even passionate opinions about the merits of various techniques and tools.

Software download sites

For almost any task you can do by using software, there are freeware or cheap shareware programs that can do it. Of course, most of these are not as sophisticated as their commercial counterparts, but some are surprisingly powerful. Using low-priced or free tools is a tradition in the Web world, so before spending big money on the latest high-profile commercial software package, check out some of the offerings at free download sites such as Tucows (`http://www.tucows.com`), Download.com (`http://www.download.com`) or the Web Tools Download Page (`http://WebDevelopersJournal.com/software/webtools.html`).

Discussion groups and mailing lists

There are literally thousands and thousands of Internet-based discussion forums, in which people discuss every topic imaginable. Naturally, many discussion forums deal with Internet development, from general Web-design topics to more specific issues such as HTML, CSS, Web graphics, Web audio, and much more.

A discussion group may be *Web-based* (sometimes called an online forum), or `email-based` (sometimes called a discussion list or a listserv). A Web-based group provides a Web site on which you can post questions and answers and browse through past postings. An e-mail-based group enables you to send e-mail messages to the group; your messages are then forwarded via e-mail to all members of the list.

Discussion groups are great when you need help with a specific problem. No matter how obscure or inexplicable your problem is, there's sure to be another Web designer out there who has dealt with it before and can offer you informed advice. Sometimes you don't even need to post your question. If a particular group lets you browse past postings, you may find that your question has been asked before and elicited a useful answer or even provoked a lengthy debate among proponents of various solutions. The best groups provide a list of Frequently Asked Questions (FAQs), which summarizes issues that have been discussed in the group in the past.

With all the free help that's available, ignorance is no excuse. So go out there and start turning out good-quality Web sites. I sincerely hope you have fun, make money, and leave the World Wide Web an even better place than you found it.

Done!

REVIEW

In this session, we have discussed some good things for you to keep in mind as you continue your study of Web-site design:

- Secrets of quality Web design
- Using existing sites as models for your own pages
- Finding resources for further study

QUIZ YOURSELF

1. What is the most important design principle of all? (See "Principles of Quality Web Design.")

2. What are three drawbacks of complex graphics and other fancy page elements? (See "Principles of Quality Web Design.")

3. When viewing a Web page in a browser, what sequence of commands reveals the HTML source code of the page? (See "The Sincerest Form of Flattery.")

4. Is it okay to copy other people's Web pages for your own use? (See "The Sincerest Form of Flattery.")

5. What are the two types of discussion forums, and how do they differ? (See "Discussion Groups and Mailing Lists.")

Sunday Afternoon

1. What is involved in troubleshooting a Web page?

2. What is the comment tag used for?

3. What does a well-written TITLE tag include?

4. What tags do search engines examine when indexing your site?

5. What do you call the file that keeps a record of every file request to a Web server?

6. Describe the process that occurs when a user requests a dynamically generated Web page.

7. Name at least two reasons why a site might want to use dynamic page generation.

8. What's the simplest way to insert an external file into an HTML page?

9. What is the result of the following SSI?

   ```
   <!--#include virtual="dogfish.html"-->
   ```

10. What are the two most popular commercial scripting solutions? Is there a free alternative?

11. What are two criteria you might use when critiquing a Web page?

12. What are three ways to divide a Web page into sections?

13. Of these three ways, which is usually the best choice for positioning elements on a page?

14. Why might a site choose to have a consistent navbar on every page?

15. Name three techniques you can use to create a navbar.

16. What design principle is the most important of all?

17. Why should you be sparing in your use of graphics, scripting, and other *cool* site features?

18. What sequence of browser commands shows you the HTML source code of a Web page?

19. Under what circumstances is it acceptable to copy code from existing Web pages for your own use?

20. What's the difference between the two types of discussion forums?

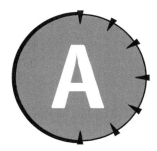

APPENDIX

A

Answers to Part Reviews

Following are the answers to the reviews at the end of each part of the book.

Friday Evening Review Answers

1. Web pages are built using HyperText Markup Language (HTML).
2. You need a Web browser to view Web pages and some type of Web editor to create and edit them.
3. A Web page is viewed using a Web browser, which displays the content of the page. Editing the file reveals the underlying HTML code, including both text content and instructions for presentation (HTML tags).
4. The three types of Web editors are text, HTML, and WYSIWYG.
5. The beginning designer should use a simple text editor; typing HTML tags manually results in better retention of what you learn.
6. The Head section of an HTML document contains a TITLE element and other optional elements, none of which are displayed on the Web page.
7. The Body section of an HTML document contains the content of the Web page.
8. Create a set of four line breaks by using four BR tags as follows:

```
<BR><BR><BR><BR>
```

9. The standard way to set off a new paragraph in an HTML document is by using a double line break. This is done with the Paragraph (P) tag.

10. If a Paragraph tag directly follows a Heading tag, a double line break appears between the two elements.

11. A Web site is a group of computer files stored on a Web server.

12. An Internet-access account allows you to view existing Web content; a Web- hosting account allows you to make your own Web content available to the public.

13. A Uniform Resource Locator (URL) is the address that allows a user to find a particular Web page. A Web address contains a header identifying the network protocol to be used (http:// for all Web addresses), the domain name of the Web server, and the filename and directory path of the file.

14. A domain name is an alphanumeric name that identifies a particular Web server.

15. Files are transferred to and from a Web server by using File Transfer Protocol (FTP). This requires a piece of software called an FTP client.

16. The Anchor (A) tag is used to define a hyperlink.

17. The HREF attribute of the Anchor (A) tag defines the destination of the hyperlink.

18. Never begin or end hyperlinked text with a space or line break; some browsers display the space as an unsightly "tick."

19. A hyperlink can refer to a Web site, an individual HTML file within a Web site, or a named location within an HTML file.

20. You can define a named location within a file by using the Anchor (A) tag. You give a name to the location by using the NAME attribute of the Anchor tag; this location can be referred to by a hyperlink.

Saturday Morning Review Answers

1. You can create bold text by using either the B tag or the STRONG tag. You can create italic text by using either the I tag or the EM tag.

2. Generally, hyperlinks are underlined. Therefore, using underlined text as a means of emphasis is not recommended because the underlined text might be mistaken for a hyperlink.

3. You can create an ordered list by using the OL and LI tags.

4. An attribute modifies the effect of a tag according to a value that you specify. For example, the WIDTH attribute allows you to specify the width of an element.

5. If a FONT tag specifies a typeface that isn't available on the user's system, the browser tries to find the closest match among the available fonts.

6. Choosing a serif or a sans-serif font is a matter of personal taste. Sans-serif fonts are perhaps more common on the Web than they are in print media.

7. You can specify the color black within any HTML element either as "black" or "000000".

8. HTML uses a six-digit string to specify color values. This string consists of three two-digit hexadecimal (base 16) numbers.

9. The text appears two sizes smaller than the preceding text element.

10. When linking to a file within the same site, relative addressing is used.

11. The WIDTH and HEIGHT attributes of the IMG tag set aside a box into which the image loads. This allows the rest of the page to continue to load, instead of forcing it to wait until the image loads.

12. The ALT attribute should always be included in an IMG tag for three reasons: if a user's system fails to display an image for whatever reason, at least he or she can get an idea of what the image is supposed to convey; visually disabled people may not be able to see your image, but may be able to read the ALT text or to hear it by using a text-to-speech application; more recent browsers can display the ALT text in a little box when the user holds the mouse over the image.

13. Create an IMG with no border by using the following code:
    ```
    <IMG SRC="image.jpg" BORDER="0">
    ```

14. Create a hyperlinked image with no border by using the following code:
    ```
    <A HREF="link.html"><IMG SRC="image.jpg" BORDER="0"></A>
    ```

15. You can wrap text around a graphic image by using the ALIGN attribute of the IMG tag.

16. You can create a margin between an image and wrapped text by using the HSPACE and VSPACE attributes of the IMG tag.

17. The .gif, .jpg and .png formats can be used for Web images.

18. The .jpg format is preferable to the .gif format for photographs.

19. The Web-safe palette consists of 216 colors. All these colors should be displayed consistently on any system capable of at least 8-bit color (256 colors).

20. For all colors in the Web-safe palette, each two-digit hexadecimal number must have one of the following values:

    00, 33, 66, 99, CC, FF

    CC3300 represents a Web-safe color.

Saturday Afternoon Review Answers

1. Use the WIDTH attribute to set the width of a table or the width of a table cell.

2. You can express the width of a table or a table cell as either an absolute (pixel) value or a relative (percentage) value.

3. Center elements within a table cell by setting ALIGN="center".

4. Create a horizontal heading spanning several table cells by using the COLSPAN attribute of the TD tag.

5. Create a borderless table by specifying BORDER="0" within the TABLE tag.

6. Newspaper-style columns are widely used in print media because they make lengthy text content easier to read.

7. A sidebar is a vertical division of a page and is used to present information that is separate from the main text.

8. You can create a margin around the contents of a table cell by using the CELLPADDING attribute of the TABLE tag.

9. The master file for a framed page is called a frameset page, and the FRAMESET tag is its main element.

10. The main difference between tables and frames is that frames create sections of a page that scroll independently of one another.

11. Every FRAME tag needs a NAME attribute and an SRC attribute.

12. The NORESIZE attribute makes it impossible for a user to resize a frame.

13. A navbar is a sidebar that contains navigational links to the main sections of a site.

14. When a hyperlink occurs within a frame, the TARGET attribute must be included in the A tag.

15. Possible values of the TARGET attribute include _blank, _parent, _top, and _self.

16. Create a hyperlink that sends an e-mail message by specifying a target that consists of mailto: followed by an e-mail address. For example:

    ```
    <A HREF="mailto:fred@fredsfishingguide.com">Click to send email</A>
    ```

17. The ACTION attribute of the FORM tag specifies the destination to which the form data is sent.

18. The SELECT, OPTION, and TEXTAREA tags are used to present user-input fields.

19. To offer users a choice between two options on a form, a radio button is a good choice.

20. Most ISPs are cautious about letting clients put CGI scripts on their servers because CGI scripts can present a security risk.

Saturday Evening Review Answers

1. A CSS rule consists of a selector followed by a declaration.

2. A declaration consists of a property and a value, separated by a colon.

3. If a particular property is not mentioned in a style sheet, that property is displayed according to the browser's default style sheet.

4. You can apply a style sheet to a document in three ways: apply styles to an individual element by using the STYLE attribute within a tag; apply styles to an entire HTML document by including STYLE tags within the HEAD section; or apply styles to a group of documents by creating a master style sheet and including a link to that style sheet in each document.

5. To apply a style sheet called styles.css to a group of HTML documents, insert the following code in the HEAD section of each document:

    ```
    <LINK REL="stylesheet" HREF="styles.css">
    ```

6. To create a rule that applies to all text elements, use BODY as the selector.

7. A rule can contain multiple selectors separated by commas.

8. Apply styles to an individual element (an inline style) by using the STYLE attribute within a tag.

9. If two styles conflict, whichever is more specific takes precedence.

10. You can create custom styles by defining a class in a style sheet.

11. A class can be applied to any HTML element by including the CLASS attribute.

12. Any type of content can be included in a DIV element.

13. Create a division that begins 200 pixels from the top of a page by using the following two CSS rules:

    ```
    position: absolute;
    top: 200px;
    ```

14. To create a division styled according to a class named leftcolumn, use the following code:

    ```
    <DIV CLASS=" leftcolumn ">
    Content
    </DIV>
    ```

15. The z-index property controls the order of overlapping layers.

16. Every business Web site should provide full contact information, including street address, telephone number, and e-mail address.

17. The four types of file addressing are absolute, default, relative, and root.

18. The site structure is the way the site is organized from the user's perspective. The directory structure is the way the files are organized on the Web server. The two structures do not necessarily resemble each other.

19. To create a hyperlink *from* a source file that has the file path root/dir_one/file.html *to* a destination file that has the file path root/dir_two/file.html, use the following code:

    ```
    <A HREF="../dir_one/file.html">Click here</A>
    ```

20. Principles for creating an effective navigational scheme are: put content on every page; put your main content up front; use a consistent navbar; and clearly label all links.

Sunday Morning Review Answers

1. An animated `.gif` is made up of frames, each an individual `.gif` image.

2. The transparent `.gif` format isn't recommended for banners that may be placed on someone else's site, as you have no way of knowing what color background they may be displayed against.

3. The animated `.gif` format is supported by most browsers with no plug-in required; Flash requires a free plug-in. Flash animations can include audio, but animated `.gifs` cannot. Creating Flash animations requires the Flash authoring package, but animated `.gifs` can be created with various authoring tools.

4. When a user requests a file that requires a plug-in that is not installed, a dialog box pops up to inform the user of the particular plug-in required. More sophisticated sites even provide a direct link to a site where the plug-in can be downloaded.

5. Any file you might want to edit later should be saved in your graphic editor's native format as well as in its final `.gif` or `.jpg` form; `.gif` and `.jpg` files may become corrupted if you try to edit them.

6. An image map is defined by a `MAP` element, which contains one or more `AREA` elements.

7. The three key parameters of a digital audio file are the sampling rate, the bit resolution, and the number of channels.

8. CD-quality audio is 16-bit, 44,100 samples per second, and stereo.

9. Streaming is a way of delivering an audio or video file in such a way that it can begin playing before the entire file is downloaded.

10. You can use include audio in a Web page by using the Anchor (`A`) tag, or the `EMBED` tag.

11. You may offer site users a choice of different quality levels to accommodate users who have different types of Internet connections. You may also offer a choice between a downloadable file and a streaming file.

12. A media player is a software application that enables you to play audio and video. A media encoder is an application that enables you to convert audio and video files to streaming formats and to other Web-friendly formats.

13. You can apply scripting to an individual element by including scripting within a tag; you can apply scripting to an entire HTML document by including a SCRIPT element within the HEAD section; and you can apply scripting to a group of documents by creating a text file containing a script and including a link to that file in each document.

14. Three events that have to do with mouse movement are: OnClick, OnMouseOver, and OnMouseOut.

15. An HTML element must have a name, specified by the NAME attribute, before it can be manipulated by scripting.

16. OnMouseOver="button.src='image2.gif'": when the mouse is over the element button, its SRC attribute has the value image2.gif; thus, the file image2.gif is displayed.

17. Use the following JavaScript code to cause a sound file to play:

OnMouseOver = "javascript:document.name.play()"

name is the NAME of the element that refers to the sound file.

18. Before deciding whether to include any scripting or other advanced technique in your Web site, ask yourself whether it adds to the usefulness of the site.

19. Client-side scripting is commonly used for redirection, browser checking, form validation, and password protection.

20. Dynamic HTML refers to the combination of HTML, CSS, and scripting.

Sunday Afternoon Review Answers

1. Troubleshooting a Web site consists of breaking a process down into its component to see which step is causing a problem.

2. The Comment tag is used to insert text into an HTML file. Text contained in the Comment tag doesn't affect the Web page. Use it to include explanatory remarks in your code, to keep a record of file revisions, and to hide code such as scripting and style sheets from non-supporting browsers.

3. A well-written TITLE tag includes the name of the page, the name of the site to which the page belongs, and a very brief description of the page's contents.

4. Search engines use the TITLE tag, the META "description" tag and the META "keywords" tag to index a site.

5. The file that keeps a record of file requests to a Web server is the server log file.

6. When a user requests a dynamically generated Web page, a script is triggered, the script assembles a Web page from various components, and the page is delivered to the user.

7. Reasons to use dynamic page generation are efficiency, database integration, personalization, and user-created content.

8. The simplest way to insert an external file into an HTML page is by using Server-side Includes.

9. The SSI

```
<!--#include virtual="dogfish.html"-->
```

inserts the file dogfish.html at the point where the SSI appears.

10. The two most popular commercial scripting solutions are Microsoft's Active Server Pages (ASP) and Allaire's ColdFusion. PHP is a popular free alternative.

11. When critiquing a Web page, consider what can be done to improve page appearance and site usability.

12. You can divide a Web page into sections by using tables, frames, or CSS.

13. CSS is usually the best choice for positioning elements on a page.

14. Having a consistent navbar on every page reinforces the unique look of a site, shows users at a glance what's available on a site, and helps users navigate back to the home page if they get lost.

15. You can create a navbar by using HTML text, individual graphic buttons, or a single graphic element together with an image map.

16. The most important design principle is to keep the goal of your Web site in mind at all times.

17. Graphics make pages load more slowly. Scripting and other cool stuff does too, and may also cause problems with older browsers.

18. To view the HTML source code of a Web page, choose View ⇨ Source in Internet Explorer or View ⇨ Page Source in Netscape.

19. Generally, it's acceptable to copy short bits of code and to modify them for use on your site as long as you don't copy the look and feel of another site. However, it's never acceptable to copy site *content* without permission.

20. A Web-based group provides a Web site on which you can post questions and answers and browse through past postings. An e-mail-based group enables you to send e-mail messages to the group; the messages are forwarded via e-mail to all members on the list.

APPENDIX

What's on the CD-ROM?

This appendix provides information on the contents of the CD-ROM that accompanies this book.

The following programs are on this CD:

- Internet Explorer
- Microsoft Windows Media Player
- BBEdit Lite
- BBEdit demo
- Dreamweaver
- Paint Shop Pro
- Mapedit
- LeapFTP
- Web Hotspots
- Web Hotspots
- Acrobat Reader
- Self Assessment Test

Also on this book's CD-ROM are a complete example Web site, individual HTML code examples from the book, and an electronic, searchable version of the book that can be viewed with Adobe Acrobat Reader.

System Requirements

Make sure that your computer meets the minimum system requirements listed in this section. If your computer doesn't match up to most of these requirements, you may have a problem using the contents of the CD.

For Microsoft Windows 9x or Windows 2000:

- PC with a Pentium processor running at 120Mhz or faster
- At least 32MB of RAM; we recommend that you have 64MB for optimal performance
- Ethernet network interface card (NIC) or modem with a speed of at least 28,800bps
- A CD-ROM drive — double-speed (2x) or faster

For Linux:

- PC with a Pentium processor running at 90Mhz or faster
- At least 32MB of RAM; we recommend that you have 64MB for optimal performance
- Ethernet network interface card (NIC) or modem with a speed of at least 28,800bps
- A CD-ROM drive — double-speed (2x) or faster

For Macintosh:

- An iMac, iBook, or any other G3 processor-based Macintosh
- At least 32MB of RAM; we recommend that you have 64MB for optimal performance
- A CD-ROM drive — double-speed (2x) or faster

You need at least 150MB of hard drive space to install the software from this CD.

Using the CD with Microsoft Windows

To install the items from the CD to your hard drive, follow these steps:

1. Insert the CD into your computer's CD-ROM drive.
2. A window appears with the following options: Install, Explore, PDF, URLs, and Exit.

- **Install:** Installs the test engine and gives you the option to install the software supplied on the CD-ROM.
- **Explore:** Allows you to bypass the interface and view the contents of the CD-ROM.
- **PDF:** Launches PDF of *Creating Web Pages Weekend Crash Course*.
- **URLs:** Launches Web page with links from the book.
- **Exit:** Closes the AutoRun window.

If you do not have AutoRun enabled, or if the AutoRun screen doesn't appear, follow these steps to access the CD:

1. Click Start ⇨ Run.
2. In the dialog box that appears, type ***d:\setup.exe***, where *d* is the letter of your CD-ROM drive. This brings up the menu screen described previously.
3. Choose the option from the menu: Install, Explore, or Exit. (See Step 2 that precedes this set of steps for a description of these options.)

Using the CD with Linux

To install the items from the CD to your hard drive, follow these steps:

1. Log in as root.
2. Insert the CD into your computer's CD-ROM drive.
3. Mount the CD-ROM.
4. Launch a graphical file manager.

Using the CD with the Mac OS

To install the items from the CD to your hard drive, follow these steps:

1. Insert the CD into your computer's CD-ROM drive.
2. Double-click on the CD-ROM icon that appears on the desktop.

3. At this point, you can install any of the software you wish, or you can copy the sample source code files from the CD-ROM to your local hard drive.

4. If you choose to install the third-party software, carefully follow the instructions that you see on the screen after you begin the installation process.

What's on the CD

The CD-ROM contains two alternative versions of an example Web site, individual HTML code examples, applications, and an electronic version of the book. Following is a summary of the contents of the CD-ROM arranged by category.

Sample Web site

Two versions of the sample Web site (Freddy's Fishing Guide, referred to throughout the book) are on the CD. A simple version, employing only the techniques covered in the first two parts of the book, is in the `freds_fishing_guide` folder. A complex version, which includes more advanced features covered in the remaining parts, is in the `freds_fishing_guide_advanced` folder.

HTML code examples

The numbered HTML code examples in the book are on the CD in the `html_examples` folder.

Applications

The following applications are on the CD-ROM:

Browser

A browser is the client software you use to view HTML files, either on your local system or over the Internet.

- *Internet Explorer:* a Web browser for Windows 9x or later. Freeware.
  For more information: www.microsoft.com

Media player

A media player is used to view audio and video files, either on your local system or over the Internet.

- *Microsoft Windows Media Player:* for Windows 98/2000/Me. Freeware.

  For more information: www.microsoft.com

HTML editors

An HTML editor is used to create and modify HTML files by directly editing their code.

- *BBEdit Lite:* for Mac Freeware.
- *BBEdit:* for Mac Demo.

  For more information: www.bbedit.com

WYSIWYG editors

A WYSIWYG editor is used to create and modify HTML files by using a graphical desktop publishing-style interface.

- *Dreamweaver:* for Mac and Windows Trial version.

  For more information: www.macromedia.com

Graphic editor

A graphic editor is used to create and modify graphic images, which can be used in Web pages.

- *Paint Shop Pro:* for Windows Evaluation version.

  For more information: www.jasc.com

Image map editors

An image map editor is used to create image maps by using a graphical interface.

- *Mapedit:* for Mac and Windows Shareware.

  For more information: www.boutell.com

- *Web Hotspots:* for Windows Shareware.

  For more information: www.1automata.com/hotspots/

FTP client

An FTP client is used to transfer files between a local system and a server.

- *LeapFTP:* for Windows Shareware.

  For more information: www.leapware.com

Acrobat Reader

The Acrobat Reader is used to read files in Adobe's Portable Document Format (.pdf). The electronic version of this book is in .pdf format, and you will occasionally encounter it on Web sites.

- *Acrobat Reader:* for Mac and Windows Freeware.

  For more information: www.adobe.com

Electronic version of Creating Web Pages Weekend Crash Course

The complete (and searchable) text of this book is on the CD-ROM in Adobe's Portable Document Format (PDF), readable with the Adobe Acrobat Reader (also included). For more information on Adobe Acrobat Reader, go to www.adobe.com.

Self-assessment test

The self-assessment test software helps you evaluate how much you've learned from this Weekend Crash Course. It will also help you identify which sessions you've perfected, and which you may need to revisit.

Troubleshooting

If you have difficulty installing or using the CD-ROM programs, try the following solutions:

- *Turn off any anti-virus software you may have running.* Installers sometimes mimic virus activity and can make your computer incorrectly believe that it is being infected with a virus. (Be sure to turn the anti-virus software back on later.)

- *Close all running programs.* The more programs you're running, the less memory is available to other programs. Typically, installers update files and programs; if you keep other programs running, installation may not work properly.

   If you still have trouble with the CD, please call the Hungry Minds, Inc. Customer Service phone number: (800) 762-2974. Outside the United States, call (317) 572-3993. Hungry Minds, Inc. provides technical support only for installation and other general quality-control items; for technical support on the applications themselves, consult the program's vendor or author.

Index

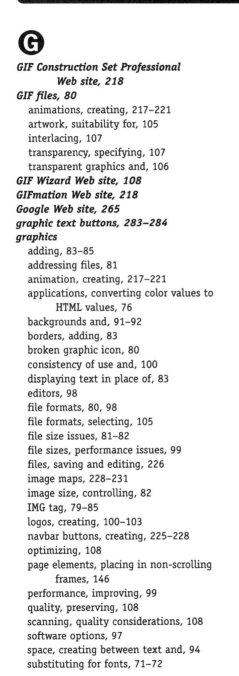

Continued

HTML (HyperText Markup Language) (continued)
- files, frames and, 137
- files, viewing, 8
- importance of, 5
- references, importance of, 55
- simple Web page listing, 6–7
- syntax compared to CSS, 176
- tags, 9–10
- tags, necessary, 17–18
- text compared to graphical text, 231
- Web pages, creating, 6–9

HTML, dynamic, 257–258

.html file extension, 7

HTML tag, 17

HTTP (HyperText Transfer Protocol), 25

http://, 31

hyperlinks
- adding to existing pages, 38–40
- Anchor tag and, 35
- coding errors, 39–40
- creating, 36–37
- cycling through, keyboard commands, 37
- formatting tags and, 38–39
- frames, 147–149
- frames, tips for, 151
- graphics, borders and, 88
- graphics, converting to, 87–88
- image map hot spots, 228
- IMG tag, 79–85
- mailto, 153
- off-site, opening in new window, 149
- pound sign (#) and, 44
- punctuation marks and, 39
- reference options, 40–46
- references, 38
- referencing locations within a page, 42–45
- referencing pages within a site, 41–42
- returning to previous page, 37
- tables of contents, creating, 45
- thumbnail graphics, linking to full size version, 89

HyperText Markup Language. *See* ***HTML***

HyperText Transfer Protocol. *See* ***HTTP***

I

I tag, 54

image maps, 228–231
- editors, 231
- navbar, 284–286

images. *See also* ***graphics***
- OnMouseOver event, 251
- troubleshooting and, 264

IMG tag, 79–80
- ALIGN attribute, 93–95
- ALT attribute, 83
- Anchor tags, nesting in, 87–88
- attributes, 82
- BORDER attribute, 83, 250
- HEIGHT attribute, 82
- HSPACE attribute, 94
- placement considerations, 94
- SCR attribute, 80
- troubleshooting, 264
- USEMAP attribute, 230
- VSPACE attribute, 94
- WIDTH attribute, 82

implementation, CSS, options, 176–178

improvements to sites, 280–281

inactive buttons, 251

indenting
- BLOCKQUOTE tag, 62
- coding style, 56

index.html, 31

inline styles, 185–186

input, validation, 258

INPUT tag, 156–157
- SIZE attribute, 157
- TYPE attribute, 156–157

interactivity
- events, 248
- rollover buttons, 248–251
- scripting and, 247–248

interlacing, graphics files, 107

international issues, extended character set, 56–59

Internet
- files, viewing, 26
- Web, 25

Continued

"

Hungry Minds, Inc.
End-User License Agreement

READ THIS. You should carefully read these terms and conditions before opening the software packet(s) included with this book ("Book"). This is a license agreement ("Agreement") between you and Hungry Minds, Inc. ("HMI"). By opening the accompanying software packet(s), you acknowledge that you have read and accept the following terms and conditions. If you do not agree and do not want to be bound by such terms and conditions, promptly return the Book and the unopened software packet(s) to the place you obtained them for a full refund.

1. **License Grant.** HMI grants to you (either an individual or entity) a nonexclusive license to use one copy of the enclosed software program(s) (collectively, the "Software") solely for your own personal or business purposes on a single computer (whether a standard computer or a workstation component of a multi-user network). The Software is in use on a computer when it is loaded into temporary memory (RAM) or installed into permanent memory (hard disk, CD-ROM, or other storage device). HMI reserves all rights not expressly granted herein.

2. **Ownership.** HMI is the owner of all right, title, and interest, including copyright, in and to the compilation of the Software recorded on the disk(s) or CD-ROM ("Software Media"). Copyright to the individual programs recorded on the Software Media is owned by the author or other authorized copyright owner of each program. Ownership of the Software and all proprietary rights relating thereto remain with HMI and its licensers.

3. **Restrictions On Use and Transfer.**

   (a) You may only (i) make one copy of the Software for backup or archival purposes, or (ii) transfer the Software to a single hard disk, provided that you keep the original for backup or archival purposes. You may not (i) rent or lease the Software, (ii) copy or reproduce the Software through a LAN or other network system or through any computer subscriber system or bulletin-board system, or (iii) modify, adapt, or create derivative works based on the Software.

   (b) You may not reverse engineer, decompile, or disassemble the Software. You may transfer the Software and user documentation on a permanent basis, provided that the transferee agrees to accept the terms and conditions of this Agreement and you retain no copies. If the Software is an update or has been updated, any transfer must include the most recent update and all prior versions.

4. **Restrictions on Use of Individual Programs.** You must follow the individual requirements and restrictions detailed for each individual program in Appendix B of this Book. These limitations are also contained in the individual license agreements recorded on the Software Media. These limitations may include a requirement that after using the program for a specified period of time, the user must pay a registration fee or discontinue use. By opening the Software packet(s), you will be agreeing to abide by the licenses and restrictions for these individual programs

that are detailed in Appendix B and on the Software Media. None of the material on this Software Media or listed in this Book may ever be redistributed, in original or modified form, for commercial purposes.

5. **Limited Warranty.**

    (a) HMI warrants that the Software and Software Media are free from defects in materials and workmanship under normal use for a period of sixty (60) days from the date of purchase of this Book. If HMI receives notification within the warranty period of defects in materials or workmanship, HMI will replace the defective Software Media.

    (b) **HMI AND THE AUTHOR OF THE BOOK DISCLAIM ALL OTHER WARRANTIES, EXPRESS OR IMPLIED, INCLUDING WITHOUT LIMITATION IMPLIED WARRANTIES OF MERCHANTABILITY AND FITNESS FOR A PARTICULAR PURPOSE, WITH RESPECT TO THE SOFTWARE, THE PROGRAMS, THE SOURCE CODE CONTAINED THEREIN, AND/OR THE TECHNIQUES DESCRIBED IN THIS BOOK. HMI DOES NOT WARRANT THAT THE FUNCTIONS CONTAINED IN THE SOFTWARE WILL MEET YOUR REQUIREMENTS OR THAT THE OPERATION OF THE SOFTWARE WILL BE ERROR FREE.**

    (c) This limited warranty gives you specific legal rights, and you may have other rights that vary from jurisdiction to jurisdiction.

6. **Remedies.**

    (a) HMI's entire liability and your exclusive remedy for defects in materials and workmanship shall be limited to replacement of the Software Media, which may be returned to HMI with a copy of your receipt at the following address: Software Media Fulfillment Department, Attn.: *Creating Web Pages Weekend Crash Course*, Hungry Minds, Inc., 10475 Crosspoint Blvd., Indianapolis, IN 46256, or call 1-800-762-2974. Please allow four to six weeks for delivery. This Limited Warranty is void if failure of the Software Media has resulted from accident, abuse, or misapplication. Any replacement Software Media will be warranted for the remainder of the original warranty period or thirty (30) days, whichever is longer.

    (b) In no event shall HMI or the author be liable for any damages whatsoever (including without limitation damages for loss of business profits, business interruption, loss of business information, or any other pecuniary loss) arising from the use of or inability to use the Book or the Software, even if HMI has been advised of the possibility of such damages.

    (c) Because some jurisdictions do not allow the exclusion or limitation of liability for consequential or incidental damages, the above limitation or exclusion may not apply to you.

7. **U.S. Government Restricted Rights.** Use, duplication, or disclosure of the Software for or on behalf of the United States of America, its agencies and/or instrumentalities (the "U.S. Government") is subject to restrictions as stated in paragraph (c)(1)(ii) of the Rights in Technical Data and Computer Software clause of DFARS 252.227-7013, or subparagraphs (c) (1) and (2) of the Commercial Computer Software - Restricted Rights clause at FAR 52.227-19, and in similar clauses in the NASA FAR supplement, as applicable.

8. **General.** This Agreement constitutes the entire understanding of the parties and revokes and supersedes all prior agreements, oral or written, between them and may not be modified or amended except in a writing signed by both parties hereto that specifically refers to this Agreement. This Agreement shall take precedence over any other documents that may be in conflict herewith. If any one or more provisions contained in this Agreement are held by any court or tribunal to be invalid, illegal, or otherwise unenforceable, each and every other provision shall remain in full force and effect.

CD-ROM Installation Instructions

The sample HTML files from each session are on the CD-ROM in the html_examples folder. You can use your Web browser to view these files directly from the CD-ROM, but I recommend copying them to a directory on your hard drive so you can edit them to experiment with various HTML techniques.

Each of the third-party programs is in its own folder. Simply run the provided setup program, and follow the instructions. See Appendix B for further information.

The directory named Self-Assessment Test contains the installation program Setup_st.exe. With the book's CD-ROM in the drive, open the Self-Assessment Test directory, and double-click the program icon for Setup_st.exe to install the self-assessment software and run the tests. The self-assessment software requires that the CD-ROM remain in the drive while the tests are running.

CSS

```
<DIV class="___">
    everything in here affected
</DIV>

<P class="___">
    only single paragraph affected

16 pt seems to be default size
```